THE AUSTRALIAN
Women's Weekly

Whether in Morocco, Lebanon, Turkey, Egypt, Tunisia or anywhere in and around the Middle East, you discover an intense love of cooking, eating and hospitality. A great many dishes are common to each country; traditions intermingle and the cultures are similar, so the food itself, while distinctively delicious, can be considered one fascinating and inspirational cuisine. Here is a superb cross-section, easily translating recipes from this region to your own table.

Pamela Clark

Food Director

CONTENTS

tahini dip

1 Place unpeeled garlic cloves on oven tray, bake, uncovered, in hot oven about 10 minutes or until garlic is soft; cool. Remove skin from cloves.
2 Blend or process garlic, cumin, rind and tahini until combined.
3 Add combined juice and water gradually in a thin stream while motor is operating, process until combined. Spoon into serving bowl, sprinkle with a little extra ground cumin, serve with toasted pitta bread, if desired.

makes about 1½ cups (375ml)

12 cloves garlic
2 teaspoons ground cumin
1 teaspoon grated lemon rind
⅔ cup (160ml) tahini
½ cup (125ml) lemon juice
½ cup (125ml) water

Process garlic, cumin, rind and tahini until well combined.

Pour combined juice and water into processor while motor is operating.

broad bean dip

1 Heat 1 tablespoon of the oil in pan, add onion, garlic, cumin and pepper, cook, stirring, until onion is soft. Add beans, cook, stirring, 5 minutes.
2 Blend or process bean mixture, remaining oil, water and lemon juice until well combined.
3 Return bean mixture to same pan, stir over heat until heated through; stir in dill. Sprinkle warm dip with a little extra cayenne pepper, if desired. Serve with vegetable sticks.

makes about 2 cups (500ml)

⅓ cup (80ml) olive oil

1 medium onion (150g), finely chopped

1 clove garlic, crushed

1 teaspoon ground cumin

pinch cayenne pepper

500g frozen broad beans, thawed, peeled

¾ cup (180ml) water

1 tablespoon lemon juice

1 tablespoon chopped fresh dill

Cook onion, garlic and spices until onion is soft.

Place bean mixture, remaining oil, water and juice in processor.

Remove skin from baked eggplants, using fingers.

Process eggplant with remaining ingredients until combined.

baba ghanoush

2 large eggplants (1kg)

¼ cup (60ml) plain yogurt

2 tablespoons lemon juice

1 clove garlic, crushed

¼ cup (60ml) tahini

2 teaspoons ground cumin

⅓ cup fresh coriander leaves

1 Pierce eggplants in several places with a skewer. Place whole eggplants on oven tray. Bake, uncovered, in hot oven about 1 hour or until soft; cool 15 minutes.

2 Peel eggplants, chop flesh roughly; discard skins.

3 Blend or process eggplant flesh with yogurt, juice, garlic, tahini, cumin and coriander until combined. Sprinkle with chopped parsley and serve with pitta bread, if desired.

makes about 2¼ cups (560ml)

Process onion mixture and remaining ingredients until smooth.

Sprinkle seasoning on triangles; toast in hot oven until crisp.

hummus

1 Heat oil in pan, add onion and garlic, cook, stirring, until onion is soft. Add cumin, cook, stirring, until fragrant; cool 5 minutes.
2 Blend or process onion mixture, chickpeas, tahini, juice, coriander, paprika and buttermilk until smooth. Spoon into serving bowl, drizzle with a little extra olive oil, if desired. Serve with spicy lavash.

spicy lavash Cut each lavash into 16 triangles, place in single layer on oven trays; sprinkle with seasoning. Toast in hot oven about 5 minutes or until crisp.

makes about 1 litre (4 cups)

2 teaspoons olive oil

1 medium onion (150g), chopped

2 cloves garlic, crushed

1½ teaspoons ground cumin

2 x 425g cans chickpeas, rinsed, drained

½ cup (125ml) tahini

½ cup (125ml) lemon juice

1 tablespoon fresh coriander leaves

1 teaspoon ground hot paprika

¾ cup (180ml) buttermilk

SPICY LAVASH

480g packet lavash

2 tablespoons cajun seasoning

cheese crescent pastries

80g butter, melted

⅓ cup (80ml) olive oil

¼ cup (60ml) water

2 cups (300g) plain flour

1 egg, lightly beaten

FILLING

1 cup (200g) grated firm fetta cheese

2 hard-boiled eggs, chopped

2 tablespoons finely chopped fresh parsley

40g packaged cream cheese

1 Combine butter, oil and water in bowl. Add sifted flour, 1 tablespoon at a time, stirring to a smooth paste between additions. Continue adding flour until a soft dough is formed.

2 Turn dough onto lightly floured surface, knead gently until smooth. Cover, refrigerate 1 hour.

3 Divide pastry in half, roll each half between sheets of lightly floured baking paper until as thin as possible (pastry should be paper-thin and almost see-through). Cover, refrigerate 30 minutes. Cut 8cm rounds from pastry, re-roll pastry scraps. Refrigerate pastry between rolling if it becomes too soft to handle.

4 Drop slightly rounded teaspoons of filling into centre of each round. Fold over and pinch edges together decoratively to seal. Place pastries on greased oven trays, brush with egg. Bake in moderately hot oven about 15 minutes or until lightly browned.

filling Combine all ingredients in bowl; mix well.

makes about 45

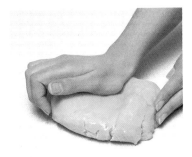

Gently knead dough on lightly floured surface until smooth.

Place filling in centre of pastry; fold over and pinch edges together.

spicy lamb pizzas

1 Combine yeast, sugar and ¼ cup (60ml) of the water in small bowl, cover, stand in warm place about 20 minutes or until mixture is frothy.
2 Sift flour and salt into bowl. Stir in remaining water, yeast mixture and oil; mix to a soft dough. Knead dough on floured surface about 5 minutes or until smooth and elastic.
3 Place dough in oiled bowl, cover, stand in warm place about 1 hour or until dough has doubled in size. Turn dough onto lightly floured surface, knead until smooth. Divide dough into 18 pieces, roll each to a 10cm round.
4 Place rounds onto greased oven trays, top each with a tablespoon of lamb topping, leaving a 1cm border. Sprinkle with nuts; brush edges with a little extra oil. Bake in moderately hot oven about 15 minutes or until cooked and browned. Sprinkle with coriander.

lamb topping Heat oil in pan, add lamb, cook, stirring, until browned; remove from pan. Add onion, garlic, spices, sambal oelek and zucchini to same pan, cook, stirring, until onion is soft. Return lamb to pan, add paste and tomato, cook, stirring, about 5 minutes or until thickened slightly; cool.

makes 18

1 teaspoon dried yeast

½ teaspoon sugar

⅔ cup (160ml) warm water

1½ cups (225g) plain flour

½ teaspoon salt

¼ cup (60ml) olive oil

2 tablespoons pine nuts, toasted

1 tablespoon chopped fresh coriander leaves

LAMB TOPPING

2 teaspoons olive oil

250g minced lamb

1 small onion (80g), finely chopped

1 clove garlic, crushed

½ teaspoon ground cinnamon

1 teaspoon ground cumin

½ teaspoon sambal oelek

1 small zucchini (90g), grated

2 tablespoons tomato paste

1 large tomato (250g), finely chopped

Combine yeast, sugar and water; stand 20 minutes or until frothy.

Divide dough into 18 pieces; roll each portion to a 10cm round.

Put 1 tablespoon lamb topping on each round, leaving a 1cm border.

11

mushroom spinach cigars

1 Heat oil in pan, add onions, garlic and spices, cook, stirring, until fragrant. Add mushrooms, cook, stirring, 5 minutes or until liquid has evaporated.

2 Stir in spinach and juice, cook, stirring, about 3 minutes or until spinach is wilted and any liquid has evaporated; cool to room temperature.

3 To prevent pastry from drying out, cover with baking paper then a damp tea towel. Layer three sheets of pastry together, brushing each with a little butter. Cut layered sheets into eight squares. Place 1 tablespoon of mushroom mixture along one end of each square. Roll pastry over filling, fold in sides, roll up. Repeat with remaining pastry, more butter and remaining mushroom mixture.

4 Place cigars about 2cm apart on greased oven tray, brush with more butter. Bake in hot oven about 10 minutes or until browned.

makes 16

2 tablespoons olive oil

2 small red onions (200g), finely chopped

2 cloves garlic, crushed

1 teaspoon ground cinnamon

½ teaspoon ground allspice

½ teaspoon ground coriander

2 large flat mushrooms (250g), finely chopped

250g spinach, finely shredded

2 teaspoons lemon juice

6 sheets fillo pastry

50g butter, melted

Cook onion, garlic and spices until fragrant; stir in mushrooms.

Place filling along one end of pastry; roll up over filling.

Place a spoonful of mixture at the end of each strip of pastry.

minted beef and pine nut pastries

2 teaspoons olive oil

1 small onion (80g), chopped

2 cloves garlic, crushed

1 teaspoon ground cumin

1 teaspoon ground coriander

300g minced beef

2 tablespoons chopped fresh mint

2 tablespoons pine nuts

2 medium potatoes (400g), chopped

½ cup (60g) grated tasty cheddar cheese

10 sheets fillo pastry

125g butter, melted

TOMATO SAUCE

2 teaspoons olive oil

1 small onion (80g), chopped

2 cloves garlic, crushed

425g can tomatoes

1 tablespoon tomato paste

2 teaspoons brown sugar

2 tablespoons chopped fresh mint

1 Heat oil in pan, add onion, garlic and spices, cook, stirring, until onion is soft. Add beef, mint and nuts, cook, stirring, until beef is browned.

2 Boil, steam or microwave potatoes until soft. Mash potatoes until smooth, add cheese; mix well. Combine beef mixture and potatoes in bowl; mix well.

3 To prevent pastry from drying out, cover with baking paper then a damp tea towel. Layer two sheets of pastry together, brushing each with butter. Cut layered sheets into three strips lengthways. Place a slightly rounded tablespoon of mixture at one end of each strip.

4 Fold one corner end of pastry diagonally across filling to other edge to form a triangle. Continue folding to end of strip, retaining triangular shape. Repeat with remaining pastry, more butter and remaining mixture. Place triangles on greased oven trays, brush with more butter. Bake in moderately hot oven about 8 minutes or until browned. Serve with tomato sauce.

tomato sauce Heat oil in pan, add onion and garlic, cook, stirring, until onion is soft. Add undrained crushed tomatoes, paste, sugar and mint, simmer, uncovered, about 5 minutes or until slightly thickened.

makes 15

potato cakes with capsicum tabbouleh

1 Place potatoes between several sheets of absorbent paper, press paper to remove as much moisture as possible. Combine potatoes, onions, egg yolk, flour and coriander in bowl; mix well.

2 Heat oil in pan, add ⅓ cup potato mixture in batches; flatten to 10cm rounds. Cook cakes slowly until browned underneath, turn, brown other side; drain on absorbent paper, keep warm. Serve topped with capsicum tabbouleh; drizzle with dressing.

capsicum tabbouleh Quarter capsicums, remove seeds and membranes. Grill capsicums, skin side up, until skin blisters and blackens; peel away skin, chop capsicums finely. Place burghul in small heatproof bowl, cover with boiling water, stand 20 minutes, drain. Place burghul between several sheets of absorbent paper, press paper to remove as much moisture as possible. Transfer burghul to bowl, add capsicums, parsley, oil and juice; mix well.

dressing Combine all ingredients in bowl; mix well.

serves 6

2 large old potatoes (600g), peeled, grated

3 green onions, finely chopped

1 egg yolk

¼ cup (30g) soya flour

1 teaspoon ground coriander

vegetable oil for shallow-frying

CAPSICUM TABBOULEH

1 medium yellow capsicum (200g)

1 medium red capsicum (200g)

⅓ cup (55g) burghul

1½ cups finely chopped fresh parsley

⅓ cup (80ml) olive oil

¼ cup (60ml) lemon juice

DRESSING

1 cup (250ml) plain yogurt

2 teaspoons ground cumin

¾ teaspoon ground turmeric

1 teaspoon sugar

Cook flattened rounds of potato mixture until brown both sides.

Peel blackened skin from grilled capsicums; finely chop flesh.

Combine soaked burghul, capsicums and remaining ingredients.

Open quartered lemons, sprinkle surfaces with salt; reshape.

Pour in enough combined juices to completely fill jar.

preserved lemons

You will need about 10 lemons and 7 limes for this recipe.

1 Quarter lemons lengthways to within 5mm of the base.
2 Open out lemons, sprinkle cut surfaces with salt; reshape lemons.
3 Pack lemons very firmly into sterilized jar (1.5 litres/6 cup capacity), pour over enough combined juices to fill jar completely; seal jar.

To serve, remove and discard pulp from rind. Squeeze juice from rind, rinse rind well; slice thinly. Serve as part of a platter with olives, cubed fetta cheese and sprinkled with olive oil. Rind can also be used in tagines, casseroles, with fish and in salads, etc.

6 medium lemons (850g)

¼ cup (55g) coarse cooking salt

1 cup (250ml) lemon juice, approximately

1 cup (250ml) lime juice

25 (120g) packaged vine leaves in brine

2 large tomatoes (500g), sliced

1 cup (250ml) tomato puree

2 tablespoons olive oil

2 tablespoons lemon juice

1 cup (250ml) chicken stock

FILLING

1½ tablespoons olive oil

½ small onion (40g), chopped

1 clove garlic, crushed

2 tablespoons white short-grain rice

1 tablespoon raisins, chopped

½ cup (125ml) water

1 teaspoon ground cinnamon

1 teaspoon ground coriander

2 tablespoons chopped fresh coriander leaves

1½ tablespoons flaked almonds, toasted, chopped

150g minced lamb

stuffed vine leaves

1 Place vine leaves in bowl, cover with cold water, stand 5 minutes; drain. Rinse leaves under cold water; drain well. Place leaves vein side up on board, place a rounded teaspoon of filling on each leaf, roll up firmly, folding in sides to enclose filling.

2 Cover base of 25cm heavy-based pan with tomato slices. Place rolls in single layer over tomatoes, pour over combined tomato puree, oil, juice and stock. Place a plate on top of rolls to keep rolls in position during cooking. Simmer, covered, over low heat about 1 hour or until cooked through.

filling Heat oil in pan, add onion and garlic, cook, stirring, until onion is soft. Add rice and raisins, mix well. Add water and spices, simmer, uncovered, about 5 minutes or until liquid is absorbed; cool. Stir in remaining ingredients.

makes 25

Place filling on each vine leaf; roll up firmly, folding in the sides.

felafel

1 Heat olive oil in pan, add onion and garlic, cook, stirring, until onion is soft. Boil, steam or microwave potatoes until soft; drain, mash until smooth.
2 Process onion mixture, potatoes, beans, spices and parsley until smooth.
3 Drop rounded teaspoons of mixture onto baking paper-covered trays, refrigerate 1 hour. Toss felafel in flour, roll into balls; flatten slightly. Deep-fry felafel in hot vegetable oil in batches until lightly browned; drain on absorbent paper. Serve with yogurt dip.

yogurt dip Cut cucumber in half lengthways; remove seeds, finely chop cucumber. Combine cucumber with remaining ingredients in bowl; mix well.

makes about 30

1 tablespoon olive oil

1 medium onion (150g), roughly chopped

1 clove garlic, crushed

2 medium potatoes (400g), chopped

1¼ cups (185g) frozen broad beans, thawed, peeled

½ teaspoon ground cinnamon

½ teaspoon ground cumin

¼ teaspoon chilli powder

⅓ cup fresh parsley leaves

plain flour

vegetable oil for deep-frying

YOGURT DIP

1 small green cucumber (130g)

¾ cup (180ml) plain yogurt

½ teaspoon ground cumin

2 teaspoons chopped fresh mint

Process onion mix, potatoes, beans, spices and parsley until smooth.

Deep-fry floured felafel balls in batches until lightly browned.

Scoop out seeds from the cucumber with a spoon.

chickpea, lentil and bean soup

1 Heat oil in pan, add onion, garlic and spices, cook, stirring, until onion is soft.

2 Stir in peas, beans, lentils, stock, juice and mint, simmer, covered, about 20 minutes, stirring occasionally, or until lentils are tender.

3 Stir in spinach, simmer, uncovered, about 5 minutes or until spinach is just wilted.

serves 6

1 tablespoon olive oil

1 large red onion (300g), chopped

2 cloves garlic, crushed

1 teaspoon ground cumin

1 teaspoon ground turmeric

1 teaspoon ground sweet paprika

½ teaspoon ground cinnamon

2 x 425g cans chickpeas, rinsed, drained

340g can red kidney beans, rinsed, drained

½ cup (100g) red lentils

1.25 litres (5 cups) vegetable stock

¼ cup (60ml) lemon juice

⅓ cup chopped fresh mint

500g spinach, shredded

Simmer soup about 20 minutes or until lentils are tender.

Stir in spinach, simmer 5 minutes or until spinach is wilted.

Add remaining ingredients and simmer until lentils are tender.

Combine yogurt, herbs and ground coriander in a small bowl.

1 tablespoon olive oil

2 medium onions (300g), chopped

3 cloves garlic, crushed

½ teaspoon garam masala

½ teaspoon sambal oelek

¼ cup (60ml) tomato paste

12 medium tomatoes (1.5kg), peeled, seeded, chopped

1.5 litre (6 cups) vegetable stock

½ cup (100g) red lentils

2 teaspoons sugar

⅓ cup chopped fresh coriander leaves

CORIANDER YOGURT

1 cup (250ml) plain yogurt

2 tablespoons chopped fresh parsley

2 tablespoons chopped fresh coriander leaves

1 teaspoon ground coriander

tomato, lentil and coriander soup

1 Heat oil in large pan, add onions, garlic, garam masala and sambal oelek, cook over medium heat, stirring, until onions are soft.

2 Add paste, tomatoes, stock, lentils, sugar and coriander, simmer, stirring, uncovered, about 20 minutes or until lentils are tender. Serve topped with coriander yogurt.

coriander yogurt Combine all ingredients in small bowl; mix well.

serves 6

21

MAINS

chicken tagine with dates and honey

1 Cut chicken into 3cm strips. Heat 1 tablespoon of the oil in pan, add chicken in batches, cook, stirring, until browned; drain on absorbent paper.
2 Heat remaining oil in same pan, add onions, garlic and spices, cook, stirring, until onions are soft.
3 Return chicken to pan with stock and water, simmer, covered, 1 hour. Remove lid, simmer about 30 minutes or until mixture is thickened slightly and chicken is tender. Stir in dates, honey and nuts; sprinkle with fresh coriander.

serves 4 to 6

9 chicken thigh fillets (1kg)

2 tablespoons olive oil

2 medium onions (300g), finely sliced

4 cloves garlic, crushed

1 teaspoon cumin seeds

1 teaspoon ground coriander

1 teaspoon ground ginger

1 teaspoon ground turmeric

1 teaspoon ground cinnamon

½ teaspoon chilli powder

¼ teaspoon ground nutmeg

1½ cups (375ml) chicken stock

1 cup (250ml) water

½ cup (85g) seedless dates, halved

¼ cup (60ml) honey

½ cup (80g) blanched almonds, toasted

1 tablespoon chopped fresh coriander leaves

Cook strips of chicken in batches until browned.

Cook onions, garlic and spices until onions are soft.

Return chicken to pan with stock and water; simmer until tender.

beef with olives and coriander

1 Cut beef into 3cm pieces. Heat ghee in pan, add beef in batches, cook, stirring, until browned all over; drain on absorbent paper.
2 Add onions and ginger to same pan, cook, stirring, until onions are soft.
3 Return beef to pan with saffron, cumin, paprika and flour, cook, stirring, until beef is well coated in spice mixture. Stir in juice and stock, simmer, covered, about 1½ hours or until beef is tender. Just before serving, stir in coriander and olives.

serves 6

1kg beef chuck steak

50g ghee

2 medium onions (300g), finely chopped

2 teaspoons grated fresh ginger

½ teaspoon ground saffron

1 teaspoon ground cumin

1 teaspoon ground sweet paprika

1 tablespoon plain flour

¼ cup (60ml) lemon juice

2 cups (500ml) beef stock

1 tablespoon chopped fresh coriander leaves

1¼ cups (200g) seedless black olives

¾ cup (120g) seedless green olives

Cook onions and ginger until onions are soft.

Pour in juice and stock; simmer 1½ hours or until beef is tender.

Make 16 deep cuts in the lamb, push a piece of garlic into each cut.

Spread spiced yogurt evenly all over lamb with a wooden spoon.

roast lamb with spiced yogurt crust

2kg leg of lamb

4 cloves garlic, quartered

2 teaspoons ground sweet paprika

2 teaspoons ground cumin

1 teaspoon ground turmeric

1 teaspoon ground coriander

1 teaspoon ground black pepper

½ teaspoon ground cardamom

½ teaspoon saffron threads

2 teaspoons grated lemon rind

2 cups (500ml) plain yogurt

1 Makes 16 x 4cm deep cuts into lamb, press garlic into cuts.

2 Combine ground spices, saffron, rind and yogurt in bowl; mix well. Spread spiced yogurt over lamb, cover; refrigerate overnight.

3 Place lamb on wire rack in baking dish, add enough water to cover base of baking dish. Bake, uncovered, in moderate oven about 1½ hours or until crust is browned and lamb tender. Remove from oven, cover loosely with foil; stand 30 minutes before carving. Serve with char-grilled tomatoes and vegetables, if desired.

serves 6 to 8

chicken, artichoke and fetta pie

1 Place chicken in shallow ovenproof dish (1.5 litre/6 cup capacity). Pour over combined spices and stock. Bake, covered, in moderate oven about 30 minutes or until tender. Remove chicken from dish, drain, finely chop; reserve ⅓ cup (80ml) juices in dish.

2 Heat oil in pan, add leeks, cook, stirring, about 10 minutes or until leeks are lightly browned and soft. Combine chicken, leeks, reserved juices, artichokes, extra cinnamon, cheese, eggs and herbs in large bowl; mix well.

3 To prevent pastry from drying out, cover with baking paper then a damp tea towel until ready to use. Brush one sheet of pastry with some of the butter, place into greased 25cm round ovenproof dish (2.5 litre/10 cup capacity) with edges overhanging. Repeat with five more pastry sheets and more of the butter, overlapping pastry around dish.

4 Spoon chicken mixture into dish, fold overhanging edges back onto filling; brush with more butter.

5 Place one sheet of pastry over filling, brush with more butter. Repeat with remaining pastry sheets and butter, overlapping sheets around dish. Trim edges of pastry so they hang 2cm over edge of dish. Fold and tuck in overhanging pastry. Bake in moderately hot oven 20 minutes, reduce to moderate, bake about 20 minutes or until browned and heated through.

serves 6

4 chicken breast fillets (680g), halved

2 teaspoons ground cumin

1 teaspoon ground cinnamon

1 teaspoon ground turmeric

½ cup (125ml) chicken stock

2 tablespoons olive oil

2 medium leeks (700g), sliced

2 x 280g jars artichoke hearts in oil, drained, chopped

½ teaspoon ground cinnamon, extra

200g fetta cheese, crumbled

2 eggs, lightly beaten

¼ cup chopped fresh parsley

⅓ cup chopped fresh coriander leaves

12 sheets fillo pastry

80g butter, melted

Overlap pastry sheets around dish, allowing edges to overhang.

Fold the overhanging edges of pastry back over the filling.

Fold and tuck in the top layers of overhanging pastry.

Combine tuna cubes and marinade in large bowl.

Thread tuna cubes onto skewers; grill or barbecue until cooked.

marinated tuna kebabs

Soak bamboo skewers in water for several hours or overnight to prevent them from burning.

1 Cut tuna into 3cm cubes. Combine tuna and marinade in large bowl, mix well; cover, refrigerate overnight.
2 Thread tuna onto 8 skewers, grill or barbecue until cooked as desired, turning once during cooking. Serve with lemon wedges, if desired.

marinade Blend or process all ingredients until smooth.

makes 8

1kg piece of fresh tuna

MARINADE

½ cup fresh parsley sprigs

½ cup fresh coriander leaves

3 cloves garlic, bruised

1 teaspoon ground cinnamon

1 teaspoon ground cumin

1 teaspoon ground sweet paprika

1 teaspoon ground coriander

½ cup (125ml) lemon juice

¼ cup (60ml) olive oil

1 teaspoon grated lemon rind

minted veal with baby squash

1 Heat oil in pan, add veal in batches, cook until browned all over; remove.
2 Add onions, garlic and spices to same pan, cook, stirring, until onions are soft. Add rind, paste, mint, stock and veal, simmer, covered, about 30 minutes or until veal is tender.
3 Add squash, simmer, uncovered, about 10 minutes or until squash are tender. Add blended cornflour and water, stir over heat until mixture boils and thickens.

serves 6 to 8

2 tablespoons olive oil
12 veal loin chops (2kg)
2 medium onions (300g), sliced
3 cloves garlic, crushed
2 teaspoons ground turmeric
4 cardamom pods, bruised
1 teaspoon ground nutmeg
1 teaspoon grated lemon rind
1 tablespoon tomato paste
2 tablespoons chopped fresh mint
2 cups (500ml) beef stock
200g baby yellow squash, halved
1 tablespoon cornflour
2 tablespoons water

Cook veal chops in batches until browned all over.

Cook squash until tender; stir in cornflour mixture until thickened.

duck in pomegranate sauce

Because of their acidic nature, pomegranates should only be cooked in stainless steel or enamel pans to prevent discolouration.

1 Place ducks on wire rack over large baking dish. Bake, uncovered, in moderately hot oven about 1 hour or until browned and just cooked. Remove from oven, cover; stand 30 minutes.
2 Cut pomegranate in half; scoop out seeds, reserve ¼ cup (60ml) seeds. Combine remaining seeds and water in stainless steel or enamel pan, bring to boil; strain.
3 Heat oil in stainless steel or enamel pan, add onion, garlic and spices, cook, stirring, until onion is soft. Add pomegranate liquid, stock, juice, sugar and almonds, cook, stirring, over heat until mixture boils and thickens slightly.
4 Place duck on board, cut through breastbone, using poultry shears. Cut on either side of backbone; remove backbone.
5 Remove breastbone and ribcage from each half of duck. Cut each half into two pieces. Repeat with remaining duck. Grill duck, skin side up, until skin is crisp. Place duck pieces on serving plate, pour over sauce, top with reserved pomegranate seeds then chopped pistachios and coriander leaves, if desired.

serves 4 to 6

2 x No. 17 ducks
1 medium pomegranate (320g)
1 cup (250ml) water
1 tablespoon olive oil
1 medium onion (150g), sliced
2 cloves garlic, crushed
1 teaspoon ground turmeric
1 teaspoon ground cinnamon
1 teaspoon ground cumin
1 teaspoon ground coriander
1 cup (250ml) chicken stock
1 tablespoon lemon juice
¼ cup (50g) brown sugar
2 tablespoons ground almonds

Reserve ¼ cup pomegranate seeds; add remaining to pan with water.

Cut through breastbone, then cut either side of backbone.

Remove breastbone and ribcage from each half of duck.

spicy roasted poussins

1 Using poultry shears, cut along both sides of poussin backbones; remove and discard backbones.
2 Place poussins, skin side down, on board. Scrape meat away from ribcage; remove ribcage. Cut through thigh and wing joints without cutting skin.
3 Scrape meat from breastbones; remove breastbones. Cut poussins in half.
4 Combine poussins in bowl with paprika, garlic, seeds, coriander, onions, chutney and oil; mix well. Cover, refrigerate overnight.
5 Place poussins on wire rack over baking dish. Bake, uncovered, in hot oven about 30 minutes or until poussins are tender, brushing with remaining marinade several times during cooking. Serve poussins on watercress sprigs, if desired. Drizzle with vinaigrette.

vinaigrette Place all ingredients in jar; shake well.

serves 4

4 x 500g poussins

2 teaspoons ground sweet paprika

2 cloves garlic, crushed

1 teaspoon cumin seeds

2 teaspoons yellow mustard seeds

1 tablespoon chopped fresh coriander leaves

2 green onions, chopped

⅓ cup (80ml) mango chutney

2 tablespoons olive oil

VINAIGRETTE

2 tablespoons olive oil

1 tablespoon lemon juice

½ teaspoon chopped fresh rosemary

¼ teaspoon sugar

Cut down both sides of backbones; remove and discard backbones.

Scrape meat away from ribcage; remove ribcage.

Bake poussins on rack over baking dish until tender.

marinated lemony lamb kebabs

Soak bamboo skewers in water for several hours or overnight to prevent them from burning.

1 Cut lamb into 3cm cubes. Combine lamb and marinade in bowl, cover; refrigerate several hours or overnight.
2 Thread lamb onto skewers, heat oil in pan, add kebabs in batches, cook until browned all over and cooked through. Serve with couscous if desired, and tomato sauce.

marinade Process all ingredients until well combined.

tomato sauce Combine undrained crushed tomatoes with remaining ingredients in small pan, simmer, uncovered, about 5 minutes or until slightly thickened.

serves 4

1kg boneless lamb

1 tablespoon olive oil

MARINADE

2 large onions (400g), chopped

2 cloves garlic, crushed

½ cup (125ml) olive oil

¼ cup (60ml) lemon juice

1 teaspoon ground cumin

½ teaspoon ground ginger

1 teaspoon ground coriander

TOMATO SAUCE

425g can tomatoes

1 small fresh red chilli, finely chopped

½ teaspoon ground cumin

¼ teaspoon ground cinnamon

Process all marinade ingredients until well combined.

Fry kebabs in batches until browned all over and cooked through.

Cook spice-covered fillets in batches until browned both sides.

Combine couscous, oil, water and coriander; stand 5 minutes.

spiced fish with chickpeas

1 Coat fish in combined spices.
2 Heat oil in pan, add fish, cook until browned on both sides and tender. Remove fish from pan; keep warm. Discard oil.
3 Add stock, chickpeas, capsicums, coriander and juice to same pan, simmer, covered, about 10 minutes or until capsicums are soft. Serve fish on herbed couscous with chickpea mixture.

herbed couscous Place couscous in medium heatproof bowl, stir in oil, water and coriander; stand 5 minutes or until liquid is absorbed.

serves 4

4 x 150g firm white fish fillets

2 teaspoons ground turmeric

2 teaspoons ground cumin

1½ teaspoons ground cardamom

1½ tablespoons olive oil

1⅔ cups (410ml) chicken stock

2 x 300g cans chickpeas, rinsed, drained

2 medium red capsicums (400g), sliced

¼ cup chopped fresh coriander leaves

1 tablespoon lemon juice

HERBED COUSCOUS

1½ cups (300g) couscous

1 teaspoon olive oil

1½ cups (375ml) boiling water

1 tablespoon chopped fresh coriander leaves

2 tablespoons olive oil

8 chicken thigh fillets (880g), sliced

1 large onion (200g), chopped

2 cloves garlic, finely sliced

1 teaspoon ground coriander

½ teaspoon ground turmeric

¼ teaspoon cayenne pepper

4 medium tomatoes (520g), peeled, chopped

3 cups (750ml) chicken stock

1 cinnamon stick

1 medium green capsicum (200g), sliced

200g baby yellow squash, quartered

2 finger eggplants (120g), thickly sliced

½ cup (85g) raisins

¼ cup (40g) blanched almonds, toasted

2 tablespoons chopped fresh coriander leaves

COUSCOUS

1¾ cups (430ml) water

20g butter, chopped

2 cups (400g) couscous

braised chicken in tomato sauce

1 Heat oil in pan, add chicken in batches, cook until browned all over; remove from pan.

2 Add onion and garlic to same pan, cook, stirring, until onion is soft. Add ground spices, cook, stirring, until fragrant. Stir in tomatoes and stock.

3 Return chicken to pan with cinnamon stick, simmer, uncovered, about 30 minutes or until sauce has thickened slightly and chicken is tender, stirring occasionally. Add capsicum, squash and eggplants, simmer, uncovered, about 5 minutes or until vegetables are tender. Discard cinnamon stick. Serve chicken mixture on couscous, top with raisins, nuts and fresh coriander.

couscous Bring water to boil in medium pan, stir in butter and couscous; remove from heat, cover, stand about 5 minutes or until water is absorbed.

serves 6

Cook chicken slices in batches, until browned all over.

Cook onion, garlic and spices; add tomatoes and stock.

Return chicken to pan with cinnamon stick, simmer 30 minutes.

chicken pilaf with apricots

1 Heat half the ghee in large pan, add chicken in batches, cook until lightly browned all over and tender; drain.
2 Heat remaining ghee in same pan, add onions, garlic and spices, cook, stirring, until onions are soft.
3 Add apricots and rice, stir over heat until rice is coated in spice mixture. Stir in stock, simmer, covered with tight-fitting lid, 15 minutes.
4 Remove from heat, stir in chicken, stand, covered, 15 minutes. Stir in currants, peas and nuts. Top with coriander, if desired.

serves 6

60g ghee

1kg chicken thigh fillets, chopped

2 medium onions (300g), sliced

1 clove garlic, crushed

1 teaspoon ground cumin

1 teaspoon ground coriander

½ teaspoon ground turmeric

½ cup (75g) dried apricots, sliced

2 cups (400g) basmati rice

1 litre (4 cups) chicken stock

¼ cup (35g) dried currants

½ cup (60g) frozen peas

½ cup (80g) pine nuts, toasted

Cook chicken pieces in batches until lightly browned all over and tender.

Stir stock into apricot and rice mixture; simmer 15 minutes.

Remove pan from heat and stir in chicken; stand, covered, 15 minutes.

lamb and chickpea casserole

1 Combine lamb, paprika and cumin in bowl, mix well, cover; refrigerate several hours or overnight.
2 Heat ghee in pan, add lamb mixture and onions, cook, stirring, until onions are soft; stir in turmeric.
3 Add undrained crushed tomatoes and sugar, simmer, covered, about 40 minutes or until lamb is just tender. Add chickpeas and herbs, simmer, uncovered, about 10 minutes or until lamb is tender and sauce thickened slightly.

serves 4 to 6

1kg diced lamb

1 teaspoon ground sweet paprika

1 teaspoon ground cumin

50g ghee

2 large onions (400g), sliced

½ teaspoon ground turmeric

2 x 425g cans tomatoes

2 teaspoons sugar

300g can chickpeas, rinsed, drained

2 teaspoons chopped fresh thyme

1 tablespoon chopped fresh parsley

Combine lamb, paprika and cumin; cover and refrigerate.

Cook lamb mixture and onions until onions are soft.

Add canned tomatoes and sugar; simmer 40 minutes.

braised lamb and eggplant with pilaf

1 Cut eggplant into 1cm slices, place in colander, sprinkle with salt, stand 30 minutes. Rinse eggplant slices under cold water, drain on absorbent paper; chop eggplant.

2 Heat half the oil in large pan, add onion and garlic, cook, stirring, until onion is soft; remove from pan. Cut lamb into 2cm pieces. Heat remaining oil in same pan, add lamb, cook until browned all over, add spices, cook, stirring, until fragrant. Add onion mixture and water, simmer, covered, 45 minutes, stirring occasionally.

3 Add eggplant, simmer, covered, 45 minutes or until eggplant and lamb are tender.

4 Meanwhile, place rice in bowl, cover with hot water, stand until cool, rinse under cold water; drain.

5 Add stock to large heavy-based pan, bring to boil, add rice, simmer, covered with tight-fitting lid, 12 minutes. Remove from heat, stand 10 minutes. Stir in tomatoes, nuts and coriander. Serve pilaf topped with lamb and eggplant mixture.

serves 4 to 6

1 large eggplant (500g)

coarse cooking salt

2 tablespoons olive oil

1 large red onion (300g), finely chopped

3 cloves garlic, crushed

600g chopped lean lamb

½ teaspoon ground cinnamon

¼ teaspoon ground cardamom

½ teaspoon garam masala

1 teaspoon ground cumin

2 cups (500ml) water

2 cups (400g) basmati rice

3 cups (750ml) chicken stock

5 medium tomatoes (600g), peeled, seeded, chopped

1 cup (150g) unsalted roasted cashews

¼ cup chopped fresh coriander leaves

Place eggplant slices in colander, sprinkle with salt, stand 30 minutes.

Stir chopped tomatoes, nuts and coriander into cooked rice.

Brush cut surface of eggplants with olive oil; bake 40 minutes.

Stir eggplant, sugar, rice, coriander and nuts into pumpkin mixture.

eggplants with pumpkin and fetta

You will need to cook ⅓ cup (65g) rice for this recipe.

4 medium eggplants (1.2kg), halved

coarse cooking salt

¼ cup (60ml) olive oil

200g piece pumpkin, finely chopped

1 small onion (80g), finely chopped

2 cloves garlic, crushed

1 teaspoon ground cumin

2 tablespoons brown sugar

1 cup cooked long-grain rice

2 tablespoons chopped fresh coriander leaves

⅓ cup (50g) hazelnuts, toasted, chopped

100g fetta cheese, crumbled

1 Sprinkle cut surface of eggplants with salt, place on wire rack over dish, stand 30 minutes. Rinse eggplants, pat dry with absorbent paper. Brush cut surface of eggplants with half the oil, place on wire rack over baking dish. Bake, uncovered, in moderate oven about 40 minutes or until eggplants are tender; cool 10 minutes.
2 Scoop flesh from eggplants, leaving 5mm shells. Chop eggplant flesh.
3 Heat remaining oil in pan, add pumpkin, onion, garlic and cumin; cook, stirring, until pumpkin is just tender. Stir in eggplant flesh, sugar, rice, coriander and nuts.
4 Divide pumpkin mixture among eggplant shells, place on oven tray; top with cheese. Bake in moderate oven about 30 minutes or until cheese is lightly browned.

serves 4

lamb, eggplant and prune tagine

1 Cut eggplants into 1cm slices, place in colander, sprinkle with salt; stand 30 minutes. Rinse slices under cold water, drain, cut into quarters.

2 Heat oil in pan, add lamb and ground spices, cook, stirring, until lamb is browned all over; remove from pan. Add garlic and onion to pan, cook, stirring, until onion is soft. Stir in water, rind and cinnamon stick. Return lamb to pan, simmer, covered, about 1 hour or until lamb is just tender.

3 Stir in prunes, nuts, honey, coriander and eggplants, simmer, covered, 30 minutes or until eggplants are tender. Discard cinnamon stick and rind. Serve tagine sprinkled with seeds.

serves 6

2 medium (600g) eggplants

coarse cooking salt

¼ cup (60ml) olive oil

1kg diced lamb

½ teaspoon ground cinnamon

2 teaspoons ground cumin

½ teaspoon ground ginger

1 teaspoon ground turmeric

2 cloves garlic, crushed

1 large (200g) onion, finely chopped

2¾ cups (680ml) water

2 strips lemon rind

1 cinnamon stick

¾ cup (125g) seedless prunes, halved

½ cup (80g) blanched almonds, toasted

1 tablespoon honey

2 tablespoons chopped fresh coriander leaves

2 teaspoons sesame seeds, toasted

Sprinkle salt on eggplant slices in colander; stand 30 minutes.

Add eggplants and coriander to pan, simmer until eggplants are tender.

spinach, leek and cheese pastries

1 Combine spinach and water in large pan, simmer, covered, few minutes or until spinach is wilted, drain; squeeze out excess liquid.

2 Heat oil in pan, add leek, garlic and spices, cook, stirring, until leek is soft and liquid evaporated. Transfer mixture to large bowl, add spinach, herbs, nuts, cheese and eggs; mix well.

3 To prevent pastry from drying out, cover with baking paper then a damp tea towel until you are ready to use it. Layer two sheets of pastry together, brushing each with a little of the butter. Cut layered sheets in half lengthways. Place ⅓ cup spinach mixture at one end of each strip.

4 Fold one corner end of pastry diagonally across filling to other edge to form a triangle. Continue folding to end of strip, retaining triangular shape. Brush triangle with a little more butter. Repeat with remaining pastry, filling and butter. Place triangles on greased oven trays. Bake in moderately hot oven about 15 minutes or until browned.

makes 12

1kg spinach, chopped

2 tablespoons water

2 tablespoons olive oil

1 large leek (500g), chopped

4 cloves garlic, crushed

½ teaspoon ground cumin

½ teaspoon ground cinnamon

¼ cup chopped fresh dill

½ cup chopped fresh parsley

½ cup (80g) pine nuts, toasted

500g fetta cheese, crumbled

2 eggs, lightly beaten

12 sheets fillo pastry

100g butter, melted

Cook spinach until just wilted, drain; squeeze out excess liquid.

Add cheese and eggs to spinach mixture and mix together well.

Place ⅓ cup spinach mixture at one end of each strip of pastry.

spicy lamb racks with quince

1 Peel quinces, cut each quince into eight pieces; remove cores.

2 Heat oil, butter, garlic and spices in large baking dish, cook, stirring, until fragrant. Add quinces, cook, stirring, about 5 minutes or until lightly browned. Stir in wine and sugar. Bake, uncovered, in moderate oven about 45 minutes or until quinces are pale pink and lightly browned, stirring occasionally.

3 Place spicy lamb racks on top of quinces in baking dish. Bake, uncovered, in moderate oven about 15 minutes or until lamb is tender.

spicy lamb racks Combine 1 tablespoon of the oil with honey and spices in bowl; mix well. Brush lamb with spice mixture, cover; refrigerate several hours or overnight.
Heat remaining oil in pan, add lamb in batches, cook until browned all over.

serves 6

6 medium quinces (2kg)

2 tablespoons olive oil

60g butter

1 clove garlic, crushed

1 teaspoon ground cumin

1 teaspoon coriander seeds, crushed

⅔ cup (160ml) dry white wine

¼ cup (50g) brown sugar

SPICY LAMB RACKS

2 tablespoons olive oil

1 tablespoon honey

2 teaspoons ground cumin

1½ teaspoons ground coriander

1 teaspoon ground turmeric

½ teaspoon ground allspice

¼ teaspoon cayenne pepper

6 racks (1kg) lamb (3 cutlets each)

Peel quinces, cut each into eight pieces and remove cores.

Brush racks with spice mixture; cover and refrigerate overnight.

Place racks on top of quinces; bake 15 minutes until lamb is tender.

braised beef with kidney beans

1 Cut beef into 4cm pieces. Heat oil in pan, add beef in batches, cook, stirring, until browned. Transfer beef to ovenproof dish (2.5 litre/10 cup capacity).
2 Add onions to same pan, cook, stirring, until soft. Add garlic and ground spices, cook, stirring, until fragrant. Stir in undrained crushed tomatoes, stock and paste; bring to boil.
3 Pour tomato mixture over beef in dish, add bay leaves and cinnamon stick. Bake, covered, in moderately hot oven 1 hour.
4 Remove lid, bake for a further 30 minutes. Stir in potatoes and leeks. Bake, uncovered, for about 20 minutes more or until beef and potatoes are tender. Discard cinnamon and bay leaves. Stir in beans and herbs.

serves 6

1kg beef chuck steak

2 tablespoons olive oil

2 medium onions (300g), finely chopped

2 cloves garlic, finely chopped

2 teaspoons ground oregano

1 teaspoon ground turmeric

2 teaspoons ground cumin

425g can tomatoes

2 cups (500ml) beef stock

¼ cup (60ml) tomato paste

2 bay leaves

1 cinnamon stick

6 baby new potatoes (240g), halved

2 small leeks (400g), thinly sliced

290g can kidney beans, rinsed, drained

2 tablespoons chopped fresh coriander leaves

2 tablespoons chopped fresh dill

Cook beef pieces in batches, until browned; transfer to dish.

Bring tomatoes, stock, paste and spicy onion mixture to boil.

Add potatoes and leeks; bake until beef and potatoes are tender.

kibbi

1 Place burghul in bowl, cover with cold water, stand 15 minutes. Drain burghul, rinse under cold water, drain; squeeze to remove excess moisture.
2 Combine burghul with lamb, onion, allspice, oregano, olive oil and water in bowl; mix well.
3 Shape ¼ cups of lamb mixture into balls, using damp hands. Hollow out centres of meatballs, using your thumb. Place rounded teaspoons of filling into hollowed centres of meatballs. Shape meatballs into ovals, using damp hands.
4 Shallow-fry kibbi in hot oil in batches until browned all over and cooked through; drain on absorbent paper.

filling Heat oil in pan, add onion, cook, stirring, until onion is soft. Add nuts, cook, stirring, until lightly browned. Add lamb, allspice and oregano, cook, stirring, until lamb is browned. Stir in mint.

makes about 16

1 cup (160g) burghul

600g minced lamb

1 medium onion (150g), grated

1 teaspoon ground allspice

1 teaspoon ground oregano

1 tablespoon olive oil

1 tablespoon water

vegetable oil for shallow-frying

FILLING

2 teaspoons olive oil

1 small onion (80g), finely chopped

1 tablespoon pine nuts

1 tablespoon slivered almonds

100g minced lamb

½ teaspoon ground allspice

½ teaspoon ground oregano

1 tablespoon chopped fresh mint

Soak burghul in water, drain; press to remove excess moisture.

Shape mixture into balls and hollow out the centre using your thumb.

Add chopped nuts and parsley to
lamb mixture and mix well.

Cook kofta on griddle pan (or grill)
in batches until browned.

750g minced lamb

1 large onion (200g),
finely chopped

2 cloves garlic, crushed

¼ teaspoon ground cloves

¼ teaspoon ground nutmeg

¼ teaspoon ground hot paprika

½ teaspoon ground cumin

½ teaspoon ground coriander

1 teaspoon finely grated
lemon rind

¼ cup (40g) pine nuts,
finely chopped

½ cup finely chopped
fresh parsley

lamb kofta

*Soak bamboo skewers in water for several hours
or overnight to prevent them from burning.*

1 Combine lamb, onion, garlic, spices and rind in
   bowl; mix well.
2 Add nuts and parsley, mix well; cover, refrigerate
   30 minutes.
3 Roll tablespoons of mixture into ovals. Thread three
   ovals onto each skewer.
4 Cook kofta in greased heated griddle pan (or grill
   or barbecue) in batches until browned and cooked
   through.

makes about 14

spicy tomato coriander prawns

1 Shell and devein prawns, leaving tails intact. Combine spices and water in small bowl; mix well.
2 Heat oil in pan, add onions, cook, stirring, 2 minutes. Add spice mixture, cook, stirring, until fragrant.
3 Add prawns and tomatoes, cook, stirring, until prawns are just tender. Remove from heat; stir in fresh coriander.

serves 4 to 6

1kg uncooked medium prawns

2 teaspoons ground hot paprika

1 teaspoon coriander seeds, crushed

1 teaspoon ground turmeric

1 teaspoon ground cumin

1 teaspoon cracked black pepper

¼ teaspoon ground cloves

¼ teaspoon ground cardamom

¼ cup (60ml) water

1 tablespoon olive oil

2 medium onions (300g), sliced

2 large tomatoes (500g), chopped

2 tablespoons finely shredded fresh coriander leaves

Shell and devein prawns, leaving tails intact.

Heat oil in pan and cook onions 2 minutes.

Add prawns and cook until prawns are just tender.

SALADS & VEGETABLES

spicy potato and coriander salad

1 Add potatoes to pan of boiling water, simmer, uncovered, until tender; drain.
2 Heat oil in pan, add onion, garlic and ground spices, cook, stirring, until onion is soft. Add potatoes and coriander, cook, stirring, about 5 minutes or until potatoes are well coated and heated through. Combine potato mixture and dressing in bowl; mix well.

dressing Place all ingredients in jar; shake well.

serves 4 to 6

1kg baby potatoes, halved

1½ tablespoons olive oil

1 medium red onion (170g), chopped

3 cloves garlic, crushed

3 teaspoons ground cumin

1½ teaspoons ground coriander

1 teaspoon ground sweet paprika

½ teaspoon ground turmeric

¼ teaspoon ground cinnamon

½ cup chopped fresh coriander leaves

DRESSING

⅓ cup (80ml) lemon juice

¼ cup (60ml) olive oil

½ teaspoon sambal oelek

1 teaspoon sugar

¼ teaspoon cracked black pepper

Add potatoes to pan of boiling water, simmer until tender; drain.

Stir potatoes and coriander into onion mixture until well coated.

Place all dressing ingredients in a jar and shake well.

okra with baby onions and tomato

1 Trim stems from okra, taking care not to puncture pods.
2 Heat half the oil in pan, add onions, cook, stirring occasionally, about 15 minutes or until onions are browned; remove from pan.
3 Heat remaining oil in same pan, add okra, garlic and spices, cook, stirring, about 5 minutes or until okra is fragrant and lightly browned.
4 Return onions to pan with undrained crushed tomatoes and stock, simmer, uncovered, about 40 minutes, stirring occasionally, or until okra is very soft and tomato mixture is thickened.

serves 4 to 6

700g okra

¼ cup (60ml) olive oil

12 baby onions (300g), halved

2 cloves garlic, crushed

2 teaspoons ground cumin

1 teaspoon ground cinnamon

½ teaspoon ground allspice

425g can tomatoes

2 cups (500ml) chicken stock

Trim stems from okra, taking care not to puncture pods.

Cook onions, stirring occasionally, until browned; remove from pan.

Return onions to pan with tomatoes and stock; simmer until okra is soft.

fattoush

1 Brush each side of bread with combined oil and garlic, place bread on oven tray. Toast in moderately hot oven about 15 minutes or until crisp; cool. Break bread into bite-size pieces.
2 Combine cucumbers, tomatoes, capsicum, onions and herbs in bowl. Just before serving, add bread; drizzle fattoush with dressing.

dressing Place all ingredients in jar; shake well.

serves 4

2 large pitta breads

2 tablespoons olive oil

1 clove garlic, crushed

2 small green cucumbers (260g), thinly sliced

4 medium egg tomatoes (300g), quartered

1 medium red capsicum (200g), chopped

6 green onions, chopped

2 tablespoons chopped fresh parsley

1 tablespoon chopped fresh mint

DRESSING

⅓ cup (80ml) lemon juice

¼ cup (60ml) light olive oil

1 clove garlic, crushed

1 teaspoon ground sweet paprika

¼ teaspoon ground cumin

¼ teaspoon freshly ground black pepper

Brush each side of bread with oil and garlic; toast in oven until crisp.

Combine remaining ingredients; add bread, drizzle with dressing.

Soak burghul in water, drain; press to remove excess moisture.

Add remaining ingredients to burghul and gently combine.

tabbouleh

1 Cover burghul with cold water, stand 15 minutes. Drain, press as much water as possible from burghul. Place burghul in large bowl.
2 Add remaining ingredients to bowl, mix gently until combined.

serves 6 to 8

⅔ cup (110g) burghul

6 cups firmly packed fresh flat-leaf parsley, coarsely chopped

½ cup coarsely chopped fresh mint

5 large tomatoes (1.25kg), finely chopped

2 medium onions (300g), finely chopped

2 green onions, finely chopped

¾ cup (180ml) olive oil

¾ cup (180ml) lemon juice

orange, date and almond salad

1 Peel oranges thickly, remove any white pith, cut between membranes into segments.
2 Combine orange segments, apricots, almonds and mint in bowl, add syrup mixture; mix well.

syrup mixture Combine water, star anise, cinnamon, cloves and honey in small pan, simmer, uncovered, about 10 minutes or until thickened and slightly syrupy. Add figs and dates; cool. Discard star anise, cinnamon and cloves.

serves 4

4 large oranges (1.2kg)

⅓ cup (50g) dried apricots, halved

2 tablespoons blanched almonds, toasted

2 tablespoons chopped fresh mint

SYRUP MIXTURE

1 cup (250ml) water

2 star anise

1 cinnamon stick

6 cloves

2 tablespoons honey

½ cup (95g) sliced dried figs

½ cup (85g) seedless dates, halved

Simmer water, spices and honey 10 minutes until thickened.

Pour syrup mixture over combined fruit, almonds and mint.

1 small red onion (100g)

4 medium egg tomatoes (300g)

2½ cups (400g) seedless black olives

3 cups (150g) firmly packed watercress sprigs

120g rocket

¼ cup (40g) drained bottled hot red chillies

1 tablespoon chopped fresh coriander leaves

DRESSING

2 tablespoons olive oil

1 tablespoon lemon juice

¼ teaspoon sugar

½ teaspoon chopped fresh rosemary

1 teaspoon cumin seeds

2 cloves garlic, crushed

olive, tomato and chilli salad

1 Slice onion, separate into rings. Cut tomatoes into wedges.
2 Combine tomatoes, onion, olives, watercress, rocket and chillies in bowl; mix well. Drizzle with dressing; top with coriander.

dressing Place all ingredients in jar; shake well.

serves 6

Slice onion into rings, cut tomatoes into wedges.

Combine salad ingredients, drizzle with dressing; top with coriander.

Cut cucumbers in half lengthways, scoop out seeds.

Combine cucumbers with remaining ingredients; refrigerate.

cucumber with minted yogurt

1 Halve cucumbers lengthways, scoop out seeds. Finely chop cucumbers.
2 Combine cucumbers with remaining ingredients in bowl, cover; refrigerate at least 1 hour before serving.

serves 4 to 6

4 small green cucumbers (500g)

2 cups (500ml) plain yogurt

¼ cup chopped fresh mint

1 clove garlic, crushed

½ teaspoon ground cumin

1 tablespoon lemon juice

tomato, fetta and green onion salad

1 Cut cheese into 1cm pieces. Cut tomatoes into wedges, remove seeds and cores; chop tomatoes finely.
2 Whisk oil and juice in small bowl until combined; add onions and mint; mix well.
3 Combine half mint mixture with tomatoes in bowl; gently stir to combine. Combine remaining mint mixture with cheese in separate bowl; gently stir to combine. Refrigerate tomato mixture and cheese mixture, covered, at least 1 hour. Place cheese mixture on serving plate, sprinkle with half the topping, top with tomato mixture, then remaining topping.

topping Finely chop nuts and seeds; combine well.

serves 4 to 6

500g fetta cheese

4 medium (500g) tomatoes

⅓ cup (80ml) olive oil

¼ cup (60ml) lemon juice

3 green onions, finely chopped

2 tablespoons chopped fresh mint

TOPPING

2 tablespoons roughly chopped walnuts, toasted

3 teaspoons sesame seeds, toasted

¼ teaspoon cumin seeds

¼ teaspoon coriander seeds

Cut the cheese into cubes; remove tomato seeds, finely chop flesh.

Stir half mint mixture into tomato and stir remaining into cheese.

artichoke and vegetable salad

1 Cut carrots in half, then in half again lengthways.
2 Heat 1 tablespoon of the oil in pan, add onion, coriander and thyme, cook, stirring, until onion is soft.
3 Add carrots and potatoes to pan, cook, stirring, 5 minutes. Add remaining oil, wine and water, simmer, covered, about 10 minutes or until just tender. Stir in remaining ingredients.

serves 4 to 6

3 large carrots (540g)

⅓ cup (80ml) virgin olive oil

1 medium onion (150g), finely chopped

1 teaspoon coriander seeds, crushed

2 teaspoons chopped fresh thyme

4 medium potatoes (800g), quartered

½ cup (125ml) dry white wine

1 cup (250ml) water

½ medium cos lettuce, chopped

400g can artichoke hearts in brine, drained, quartered

1 tablespoon lemon juice

1 teaspoon cracked black pepper

Cut each carrot in half, then in half again lengthways.

Add onion to heated oil and cook until soft.

Add carrots and potatoes to pan; cook, stirring, 5 minutes.

Peel beetroot while still warm, then cut into wedges.

Process remaining ingredients until mint is finely chopped.

minted beetroot salad

1 Wash beetroot, trim leaves, leaving about 3cm of stem attached to beetroot. Add unpeeled beetroot to large pan of boiling water, boil, uncovered, about 45 minutes or until tender; drain.
2 Peel beetroot while warm; cut beetroot into wedges.
3 Blend or process remaining ingredients until mint is finely chopped. Serve beetroot topped with yogurt mixture.

serves 6 to 8

6 medium fresh beetroot (1kg)
1 cup (250ml) plain yogurt
1 clove garlic, chopped
1 tablespoon tahini
1½ tablespoons lemon juice
½ cup fresh mint leaves

1kg green beans

425g can tomatoes

1 tablespoon olive oil

2 cloves garlic, crushed

2 teaspoons ground cumin

2 teaspoons ground coriander

¼ teaspoon cayenne pepper

¾ cup (90g) chopped walnuts, toasted

½ cup chopped fresh coriander leaves

1 teaspoon sugar

1 small red capsicum (150g), thinly sliced

1 small yellow capsicum (150g), thinly sliced

beans with walnut tomato sauce

1 Boil, steam or microwave beans until tender; drain.
2 Blend or process undrained tomatoes until smooth.
3 Heat oil in pan, add garlic, ground spices and nuts, cook, stirring, until fragrant. Add tomatoes, fresh coriander and sugar, cook, stirring, until heated through. Remove from heat, stir in capsicum.
4 Combine beans with capsicum mixture in large bowl; mix well.

serves 6 to 8

Add tomatoes, coriander and sugar to spicy nut mixture.

Mix together cooked beans and capsicum mixture.

layered eggplant and capsicum salad

1 Quarter capsicums, remove seeds and membranes. Grill capsicums, skin side up, until skin blisters and blackens. Peel away skin, slice capsicums thickly.

2 Cut eggplants in half lengthways. Heat 1 tablespoon of the oil in pan, add a third of the eggplants to pan, cook about 10 minutes, or until browned all over and very soft; drain on absorbent paper. Repeat with remaining oil and eggplants.

3 Spread quarter of the yogurt dressing onto serving plate; top with a third of the eggplants, then a third of the capsicums. Repeat layering twice more. Top with remaining yogurt dressing; sprinkle with nuts.

yogurt dressing Combine all ingredients in bowl; mix well.

serves 6 to 8

3 medium red capsicums (600g)

1kg (about 16) finger eggplants

⅓ cup (80ml) olive oil

⅓ cup (50g) chopped pistachios, toasted

YOGURT DRESSING

1 cup (250ml) plain yogurt

1 clove garlic, crushed

¼ cup chopped fresh coriander leaves

1½ tablespoons chopped fresh oregano

1 teaspoon ground cumin

2 teaspoons honey

Peel blackened skin from capsicum pieces; slice thickly.

Cook eggplant halves in batches until browned all over and soft.

Layer yogurt dressing, eggplants and capsicums on serving plate.

GRAINS & PULSES

almond coriander couscous

1 Combine couscous and water in bowl, stand 5 minutes or until water is absorbed. Fluff couscous with fork.
2 Heat oil in large pan, add garlic and onions, cook, stirring, until onions are soft. Add couscous to pan, stir over heat until heated through.
3 Stir nuts, currants and coriander into couscous mixture.

serves 6

3 cups (600g) couscous

3 cups (750ml) boiling water

¼ cup (60ml) olive oil

1 clove garlic, crushed

2 green onions, chopped

¾ cup (105g) slivered almonds, toasted

⅓ cup (50g) dried currants

½ cup chopped fresh coriander leaves

Soak couscous in water 5 minutes until water is absorbed.

Cook garlic and onions until onions are soft; stir in couscous.

Stir nuts, currants and coriander into couscous mixture.

74

fruity rice

1 Heat ghee in medium heavy-based pan, add rice, cook,
   stirring, until rice is coated with ghee. Add water, simmer,
   covered with tight-fitting lid, 12 minutes. Remove pan
   from heat, stand, covered, 10 minutes.
2 Add remaining ingredients to rice mixture and stir well.

serves 4 to 6

50g ghee

1½ cups (300g) basmati rice

3 cups (750ml) water

250g fresh dates, seeded,
thinly sliced

2 teaspoons orange flower
water

½ cup (75g) dried apricots,
thinly sliced

2 tablespoons chopped
fresh parsley

*Stir rice into melted ghee until
well coated; add water and simmer.*

*Add remaining ingredients to rice
mixture and stir well.*

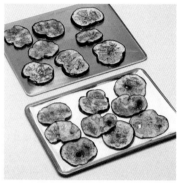

Grill oiled slices of eggplant until lightly browned on both sides.

spicy vegetables with chickpeas

1 Cut eggplants into 1cm slices, place in colander, sprinkle with salt, stand 30 minutes. Rinse slices under cold water, drain, pat dry with absorbent paper. Brush slices with half the oil, place in single layer on oven trays, grill on both sides until lightly browned; drain on absorbent paper. Cut slices in half.

2 Heat remaining oil in pan, add leek, garlic and spices, cook, stirring, until leek is soft. Add undrained crushed tomatoes, chickpeas, vegetables, nuts, herbs and stock, simmer, covered, until vegetables are tender.

3 Add spinach and eggplants to vegetable mixture, simmer, covered, about 5 minutes or until spinach is wilted.

serves 6

2 large eggplants (1kg)

coarse cooking salt

⅓ cup (80ml) olive oil

1 medium leek (350g), chopped

2 cloves garlic, crushed

1 teaspoon ground cumin

1 teaspoon ground cardamom

1 teaspoon ground turmeric

1 teaspoon ground sweet paprika

½ teaspoon ground cinnamon

2 x 425g cans tomatoes

425g can chickpeas, rinsed, drained

3 small zucchini (270g), sliced

150g green beans, halved

350g baby yellow squash, halved

200g baby carrots, halved

½ cup (75g) pistachios, toasted, chopped

⅓ cup chopped fresh parsley

¼ cup chopped fresh mint

¼ cup chopped fresh coriander leaves

1½ cups (375ml) vegetable stock

500g spinach, shredded

lavash

Poppy, caraway and sesame seeds can be used in this recipe. Sometimes this dough will become too elastic and difficult to roll; in this case, cover the dough, stand for 30 minutes then continue as directed.

1 Combine yeast with honey and sugar in small bowl, stir in water, cover, stand in warm place about 15 minutes or until mixture is frothy.

2 Sift dry ingredients into large bowl. Stir in yeast mixture, mix to a firm dough. Knead dough on floured surface about 2 minutes or until dough is smooth. Place dough in oiled bowl, cover; refrigerate 45 minutes.

3 Turn dough onto floured surface, knead until smooth. Divide dough in half, roll each half into a 13cm x 60cm rectangle.

4 Prick rectangles with fork, brush lightly with egg white. Cut each rectangle into 16 triangles, sprinkle with seeds. Place triangles about 2cm apart on lightly floured oven trays. Bake in moderate oven about 10 minutes or until browned. Serve with hummus dip, if desired.

makes 32

1 teaspoon dried yeast
1 teaspoon honey
1 teaspoon sugar
½ cup (125ml) warm water
1¼ cups (185g) plain flour
2 teaspoons salt
¼ teaspoon ground hot paprika
¼ teaspoon cayenne pepper
1 egg white, lightly beaten
2 tablespoons assorted seeds

Stir frothy yeast mixture into bowl with sifted dry ingredients.

Cut each dough rectangle into 16 triangles, sprinkle with seeds.

megadarra

1 Combine lentils and water in medium pan, simmer, covered, about 25 minutes or until just tender. Add rice, extra water, spices, salt, pepper and half the caramelised onions, cook, stirring, until mixture boils. Simmer, covered, stirring occasionally, about 15 minutes or until rice is tender. Serve warm or cold, topped with remaining caramelised onions.

caramelised onions Heat oil in pan, add onions and sugar, cook, stirring, 5 minutes. Add vinegar and half the water, cook, stirring, about 10 minutes. Add remaining water, cook about 5 minutes or until onions are caramelised.

serves 4

1 cup (200g) brown lentils

2½ cups (625ml) water

½ cup (100g) white long-grain rice

3 cups (750ml) water, extra

1 teaspoon ground allspice

1 teaspoon ground coriander

1 teaspoon salt

1 teaspoon freshly ground black pepper

CARAMELISED ONIONS

¼ cup (60ml) olive oil

3 large onions (600g), halved, sliced

3 teaspoons sugar

1 tablespoon balsamic vinegar

½ cup (125ml) water

Add remaining water to caramelised onions; cook 5 minutes.

Add rice, water, spices, salt and pepper, and half the onions.

chickpeas with spinach and spices

1 Heat oil in pan, add onion, garlic and spices, cook, stirring, until onion is soft.
2 Stir in chickpeas, tomatoes, paste and dates; then stir in water and herbs, simmer, covered, about 10 minutes.
3 Stir in spinach, simmer, uncovered, about 5 minutes or until spinach is just wilted.

serves 4 to 6

2 tablespoons olive oil

1 medium onion (150g), chopped

3 cloves garlic, crushed

1 teaspoon ground cinnamon

1 teaspoon ground sweet paprika

2 teaspoons ground coriander

2 teaspoons cumin seeds

3 x 425g cans chickpeas, rinsed, drained

3 small tomatoes (300g), chopped

2 tablespoons tomato paste

¼ cup (40g) seedless chopped dates

1 cup (250ml) water

¼ cup chopped fresh coriander leaves

2 tablespoons chopped fresh mint

500g spinach, chopped

Cook onion, garlic and spices until onion is soft.

Stir in chickpeas, tomatoes, paste, dates, water and herbs; simmer.

vegetable rice with chickpeas

You will need to cook 1 cup (200g) long-grain rice for this recipe.

1 Heat oil in large pan, add onion, garlic, sambal oelek and spices, cook, stirring, until onion is soft.
2 Add undrained crushed tomatoes, squash and herbs, simmer, uncovered, until squash are tender.
3 Add rice, chickpeas and juice, cook, stirring, until heated through.

serves 6

1 tablespoon olive oil

1 large onion (200g), chopped

3 cloves garlic, crushed

1 teaspoon sambal oelek

2 teaspoons ground cumin

½ teaspoon ground cinnamon

1 teaspoon ground ginger

425g can tomatoes

150g baby yellow squash, quartered

2 tablespoons chopped fresh parsley

2 tablespoons chopped fresh coriander leaves

3 cups cooked white long-grain rice

2 x 425g cans chickpeas, rinsed, drained

¼ cup (60ml) orange juice

Cook onion, garlic, sambal oelek and spices until onion is soft.

Add tomatoes, squash and herbs, simmer until squash are tender.

Cook garlic and onion until soft; stir in saffron, rind and spices.

Stir in rice until well coated, add stock and simmer 12 minutes.

saffron orange rice with pine nuts

2 tablespoons olive oil

1 clove garlic, crushed

1 large onion (200g), chopped

¼ teaspoon saffron threads

2 teaspoons grated orange rind

½ teaspoon ground cinnamon

1 teaspoon ground cumin

2 cups (400g) basmati rice

1 litre (4 cups) chicken stock

¼ cup (35g) dried currants

2 tablespoons chopped fresh parsley

⅓ cup (50g) pine nuts, toasted

1 Heat oil in pan, add garlic and onion, cook, stirring, until onion is just soft. Add saffron, rind and spices.
2 Add rice, stir over heat until rice is coated with oil. Stir in stock, simmer, covered with tight-fitting lid, 12 minutes.
3 Remove from heat; stand, covered, 10 minutes. Stir in currants and parsley; sprinkle with nuts. Top with shredded orange rind, if desired.

serves 6

figs in honey and port wine

We used corella pears in this recipe.

1 Peel rind thinly from lemon using a vegetable peeler. Cut any white pith from rind. Cut rind into very thin strips. Combine rind, port, water, honey, cinnamon sticks, vanilla bean and peppercorns in pan, boil, uncovered, about 10 minutes or until reduced by half.
2 Add figs and pears to pan, simmer, uncovered, about 5 minutes or until fruit is just tender. Remove fruit to bowl. Simmer syrup about 10 minutes or until thickened; pour over fruit. Serve fruit mixture at room temperature with honeyed mascarpone.

honeyed mascarpone Beat egg yolks and honey in small bowl with electric mixer until thick and pale, stir in mascarpone and nutmeg.

serves 4 to 6

1 medium lemon (140g)

¼ cup (60ml) port

1½ cups (375ml) water

½ cup (125ml) honey

2 cinnamon sticks

1 vanilla bean, split

6 black peppercorns

8 medium fresh figs (500g)

2 medium pears (400g), quartered

HONEYED MASCARPONE

2 egg yolks

2 tablespoons honey

250g mascarpone cheese

½ teaspoon ground nutmeg

Boil rind, port, water, honey, cinnamon, vanilla and peppercorns.

Add figs and pears, simmer until tender; remove fruit to bowl.

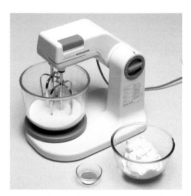
Beat yolks and honey until thick; stir in mascarpone and nutmeg.

creamed honey rice

1 Combine milk and honey in large pan, stir over heat until honey is melted; bring to boil.

2 Add rice, currants and cardamom to pan, simmer, uncovered, about 45 minutes or until rice is tender and mixture thick, stirring occasionally. Serve warm, topped with nuts. Drizzle with cream and extra honey, if desired.

serves 4 to 6

1.5 litres (6 cups) milk

¼ cup (60ml) honey

¾ cup (150g) white short-grain rice

¼ cup (35g) dried currants

1 teaspoon ground cardamom

1 tablespoon chopped unsalted cashews, toasted

1 tablespoon chopped pistachios, toasted

Stir milk and honey in large pan until honey melts; bring to boil.

Add rice, currants and cardamom, simmer until rice is tender.

semolina cake

1 Beat butter, essence and sugar in small bowl with electric mixer until light and fluffy. Add eggs one at a time, beating well between additions.
2 Stir in combined sifted semolina, baking powder and soda alternately with sour cream.
3 Spread mixture evenly into greased 20cm x 30cm lamington pan; top with nuts. Bake in moderate oven about 30 minutes. Pour hot syrup over hot cake in pan; cool in pan.

syrup Combine sugar and water in medium pan, stir over low heat, without boiling, until sugar is dissolved. Stir in juice, simmer, uncovered, without stirring, about 7 minutes or until slightly thickened (do not allow syrup to change colour).

serves 4

125g butter

1 teaspoon vanilla essence

¾ cup (150g) firmly packed brown sugar

2 eggs

2 cups (320g) semolina

1 teaspoon baking powder

½ teaspoon bicarbonate of soda

¾ cup (180ml) low-fat sour cream

⅓ cup (50g) roasted hazelnuts

SYRUP

1½ cups (330g) caster sugar

1 cup (250ml) water

2 tablespoons lemon juice

Beat butter, essence and sugar until light and fluffy; add eggs.

Spread mixture into greased lamington pan; top with nuts.

Simmer juice, water and sugar, without stirring, until thickened.

sesame honey fritters

1 Combine yeast, sugar and water in small bowl, cover; stand in warm place about 10 minutes or until frothy.

2 Sift flour and salt into medium bowl, add yeast mixture, mix to a firm dough. Knead dough on floured surface about 10 minutes or until smooth and elastic. Place dough in oiled bowl, cover, stand in warm place about 1½ hours or until dough has doubled in size.

3 Blend or process seeds until finely crushed, place in large bowl with extra sifted flour, oil, vinegar, orange flower water, egg yolk and butter; mix well.

4 Add sesame mixture to yeast mixture, mix to a soft dough. Knead dough on floured surface about 10 minutes or until smooth and elastic.

5 Roll tablespoons of dough into 16cm sausages, cut each in half. Press two ends together, twist shapes, press ends together; repeat with remaining dough. Place twists on trays, cover, stand in warm place about 30 minutes or until nearly doubled in size.

6 Deep-fry fritters in hot oil in batches for a few minutes or until browned all over; drain on absorbent paper.

7 Add honey to medium heatproof bowl, place bowl over pan of simmering water. Place hot fritters in warm honey in batches; stand 5 minutes. Drain on wire rack over tray, sprinkle with extra seeds. Serve cold.

makes about 30

2 teaspoons (7g) dried yeast

1 teaspoon sugar

⅓ cup (80ml) warm water

¾ cup (110g) plain flour

½ teaspoon salt

¾ cup (110g) sesame seeds, toasted

1¼ cups (185g) plain flour, extra

¼ cup (60ml) vegetable oil

2 tablespoons white wine vinegar

1 tablespoon orange flower water

1 egg yolk

50g butter, melted

vegetable oil for deep-frying

2 cups (500ml) honey

¼ cup (35g) sesame seeds, extra

Roll dough into sausages, cut in half; press ends together and twist.

Deep-fry fritters in hot oil in batches until browned all over, drain.

Place honey in heatproof bowl over hot water; add fritters and stand.

sesame seed brittle

1½ cups (330g) sugar

¼ cup (60ml) water

½ cup (125ml) honey

2 cups (300g) sesame seeds

1 Grease 26cm x 32cm Swiss roll pan, cover base with baking paper. Combine sugar, water and honey in medium pan, stir over heat, without boiling, until sugar is dissolved. Brush sugar crystals from side of pan with brush dipped in water.

2 Boil, uncovered, without stirring, until mixture reaches soft ball stage (116°C) on candy thermometer (a teaspoon of mixture will form a soft ball when dropped into a cup of cold water).

3 Allow bubbles to subside, gently stir in seeds. Return mixture to boil, simmer, without stirring, until mixture reaches small crack stage (138°C) on candy thermometer (syrup forms a fine thread when dropped into cold water and can be snapped with the fingers).

4 Allow bubbles to subside, pour mixture into prepared pan. Stand 10 minutes, mark into desired shapes. When cold, break into pieces.

Brush sugar crystals from side of pan with wet brush.

Boil syrup, without stirring, until mixture reaches soft ball stage.

Pour mixture into pan; cool, mark desired shapes, break up when cold.

Rub butter into flour, stir in enough water to mix to a firm dough.

Place filling in centre of pastry; fold into crescents and seal edges.

date and nut crescents

1 Sift flour into large bowl, rub in butter, gradually stir in enough water to mix to a firm dough. Knead dough on lightly floured surface about 5 minutes or until smooth, cover; refrigerate 1 hour.

2 Roll pastry on floured surface until 3mm thick, cut into 7cm rounds.

3 Brush edges of rounds with water, drop a teaspoon of filling into centre of each round, fold over to enclose filling; press edges together. Shape into crescents, place 2cm apart on greased oven trays. Bake in moderate oven about 20 minutes; cool on wire racks. Toss crescents in sifted icing sugar.

filling Combine dates and water in small pan, simmer, uncovered, about 5 minutes or until dates are softened. Stir in remaining ingredients; cool.

makes about 40

1⅔ cups (250g) plain flour

125g butter, chopped

¼ cup (60ml) iced water, approximately

icing sugar mixture

FILLING

250g (about 10) fresh dates, seeded, chopped

⅓ cup (80ml) water

¾ cup (75g) walnuts, toasted, chopped

¼ teaspoon ground cinnamon

lime pistachio sherbet

1 Combine sugar and water in medium pan, stir over heat, without boiling, until sugar is dissolved. Simmer, uncovered, without stirring, about 10 minutes or until mixture is slightly thickened; cool.

2 Stir in rind, juice and nuts, pour into lamington pan, cover with foil; freeze until firm.

3 Chop sherbet, place in large bowl with egg whites and a little colouring, beat with electric mixer until smooth. Return mixture to pan, cover with foil, freeze until firm.

4 Chop sherbet, beat in large bowl with electric mixer until smooth. Return mixture to pan, cover with foil, freeze until firm.

serves 4 to 6

1 cup (220g) sugar

2½ cups (625ml) water

2 teaspoons finely grated lime rind

1¼ cups (310ml) lime juice

¼ cup (35g) pistachios, finely chopped

2 egg whites

green food colouring

Stir lime rind and juice, and pistachios into syrup.

Beat sherbet, whites and colouring until smooth; freeze until firm.

orange almond cookies

1 Beat butter, rind, sifted icing sugar and orange flower water in small bowl with electric mixer until light and fluffy. Add eggs gradually, beat until just combined. Transfer mixture to large bowl. Stir in sifted flour and ground nuts, mix to a soft dough. Wrap dough in plastic, refrigerate 30 minutes.

2 Roll tablespoons of mixture into balls. Place balls about 4cm apart on greased oven trays, flatten slightly, press halved nuts into centres. Bake cookies in moderate oven about 15 minutes or until lightly browned. Cool cookies on trays.

makes about 45

200g butter, chopped

1 tablespoon finely grated orange rind

1 cup (160g) icing sugar mixture

2 teaspoons orange flower water

2 eggs, lightly beaten

2 cups (300g) plain flour

2½ cups (310g) ground almonds

¼ cup (40g) blanched almonds, halved

Beat butter mixture until light and fluffy; gradually pour in eggs.

Roll mixture into balls, flatten slightly and press nuts into centre.

Place half pastry over base, spread combined ricotta mixture on top.

Bake 30 minutes; pour hot syrup over pastry and cool.

konafa

375g packet kataifi shredded pastry

185g butter, melted

2 cups (400g) ricotta cheese

½ cup (60g) chopped pecans

1 cup (150g) dried apricots, chopped

½ teaspoon ground nutmeg

½ teaspoon ground ginger

½ cup (125ml) plain yogurt

2 tablespoons maple-flavoured syrup

SYRUP

1½ cups (375ml) water

1¾ cups (385g) sugar

¼ cup (60ml) maple-flavoured syrup

1 tablespoon orange flower water

1 Place pastry in large bowl, pull strands of pastry apart, pour butter over pastry, mix well.

2 Grease large shallow ovenproof dish (4 litre/16 cup capacity), line with baking paper. Place half the pastry mixture over base of prepared dish. Spread combined remaining ingredients over pastry.

3 Top with remaining pastry. Bake in moderate oven about 30 minutes or until browned. Pour hot syrup immediately over pastry, cool. Cover, refrigerate 3 hours or overnight.

syrup Combine all ingredients in medium pan, stir over heat, without boiling, until sugar is dissolved. Simmer, uncovered, without stirring, about 15 minutes or until mixture is slightly thickened.

orange coconut cake

We used sauternes in this recipe.

1. Grease deep 23cm round cake pan, line pan with baking paper. Beat butter, rind and sugar in small bowl with electric mixer until light and fluffy. Add eggs one at a time, beating well between additions.
2. Transfer mixture to large bowl. Stir in sifted flour, baking powder and cinnamon, ground almonds, coconut and pecans. Stir in juice and wine.
3. Spread mixture into prepared pan, sprinkle with flaked almonds. Bake in moderate oven about 45 minutes. Pour hot syrup over hot cake in pan. Cool in pan.

   syrup Combine sugar and juice in pan, stir over low heat, without boiling, until sugar is dissolved. Boil, uncovered, without stirring, about 5 minutes or until syrup is slightly thickened.

250g butter, chopped

1 tablespoon grated orange rind

¼ cup (55g) caster sugar

4 eggs

1 cup (150g) self-raising flour

¼ teaspoon baking powder

2 teaspoons ground cinnamon

1 cup (125g) ground almonds

1½ cups (135g) coconut

½ cup (60g) chopped pecans

½ cup (125ml) orange juice

¼ cup (60ml) sweet white wine

¼ cup (20g) flaked almonds

SYRUP

1 cup (220g) caster sugar

⅔ cup (160ml) orange juice

Beat butter, rind and sugar until light and fluffy; add eggs.

Once sugar dissolves in juice, boil, without stirring, until thickened.

baked spiced quinces

6 medium quinces (2kg)

1 medium orange (180g)

1 litre (4 cups) boiling water

2 cups (440g) caster sugar

2 vanilla beans, split

4 cardamom pods, crushed

1 cinnamon stick

1 tablespoon honey

½ cup (125ml) orange juice

1 Peel and halve quinces, cut each half into four pieces; remove core.
2 Peel four thin pieces of rind from orange using a vegetable peeler. Cut pieces of rind into very thin strips.
3 Combine boiling water and sugar in jug, stir until sugar is dissolved. Place quinces in large shallow ovenproof dish (4.5 litre/18 cup capacity). Add rind, vanilla beans, cardamom and cinnamon. Pour sugar syrup over quinces.
4 Bake quinces, covered, in moderately hot oven about 2 hours or until quinces are changed in colour, tender and liquid is syrupy. Carefully remove quinces to large bowl. Stir honey and juice into syrup mixture in dish; pour over quinces in bowl, cover; refrigerate 3 hours or overnight. Remove cinnamon and vanilla beans.

serves 6 to 8

Peel and halve quinces, cut each half into four pieces; remove core.

Remove white pith from rind; cut into thin strips.

Pour sugar syrup over quinces, rind, vanilla beans and spices.

baklava

1 Combine all the nuts, sugar and cinnamon in bowl.
2 Grease 20cm x 30cm lamington pan with a little of the ghee.
   Layer three pastry sheets together, brushing each with a little
   more ghee. Fold layered sheets in half, press into pan.
3 Sprinkle with one-third of the nut mixture. Continue layering
   with remaining pastry, more ghee and nut mixture, ending
   with pastry. Trim pastry edge to fit pan.
4 Cut five strips lengthways through layered pastry, cut each
   strip into five diamonds. Pour over any remaining ghee. Bake
   in moderate oven 30 minutes, reduce heat to slow, bake about
   10 minutes or until browned. Pour hot orange syrup over hot
   baklava; cool in pan.

orange syrup Combine all ingredients in medium pan; stir over
low heat, without boiling, until sugar is dissolved. Simmer,
uncovered, without stirring, about 5 minutes or until syrupy.

1½ cups (165g) packaged
ground hazelnuts

1 cup (125g) finely chopped
hazelnuts

⅓ cup (75g) caster sugar

1 teaspoon ground cinnamon

180g ghee, melted

12 sheets fillo pastry

ORANGE SYRUP

1 cup (220g) caster sugar

⅔ cup (160ml) water

1 teaspoon grated orange rind

½ teaspoon ground cinnamon

*Fold layered pastry sheets in half
and press into pan.*

*Sprinkle one-third nut mixture on
pastry; continue layering.*

*Pour hot orange syrup over hot,
freshly baked baklava.*

poppy seed cookies

200g butter, chopped

2 teaspoons grated lime rind

⅓ cup (75g) caster sugar

½ teaspoon ground cinnamon

2 teaspoons lime juice

1 tablespoon poppy seeds

1¾ cups (260g) plain flour

¼ cup (35g) macadamia nuts, quartered

1 Beat butter, rind, sugar and cinnamon in small bowl with electric mixer until just combined. Stir in juice and seeds, then sifted flour in two batches.
2 Divide mixture in half, roll each piece on floured surface to an 18cm sausage. Wrap in plastic, refrigerate until firm. Trim ends, cut into 8mm slices.
3 Place cookies about 2cm apart on greased oven trays; press nuts into centres. Bake in moderate oven about 12 minutes or until lightly browned. Stand 5 minutes, cool on wire racks.

makes about 48

Stir juice and seeds into butter mixture; stir in flour in batches.

Roll dough into two 18cm sausages; wrap in plastic and refrigerate.

Place cookies on oven trays, press macadamias into centres; bake.

Brush sugar crystals from side of pan while syrup simmers to 116°C.

Simmer syrup and cornflour mixture until translucent and pale.

turkish delight

4 cups (880g) caster sugar

1 litre (4 cups) water

1 teaspoon lemon juice

1 cup (150g) cornflour

1 teaspoon cream of tartar

1½ tablespoons rosewater

red food colouring

¾ cup (120g) pure icing sugar

¼ cup (35g) cornflour, extra

1 Combine sugar, 1½ cups (375ml) of the water and juice in pan, stir over low heat, without boiling, until sugar is dissolved. Brush sugar crystals from side of pan with brush dipped in water. Simmer, uncovered, without stirring, until mixture reaches soft ball stage (116°C) on candy thermometer (a teaspoon of mixture will form a soft ball when dropped into cold water). Remove from heat.

2 Meanwhile, in separate medium heavy-based pan, blend cornflour and cream of tartar with enough of the remaining water to make a smooth paste. Stir in remaining water, whisk constantly over heat until mixture boils and thickens.

3 Gradually pour hot syrup in a thin stream into cornflour mixture, whisking constantly. Simmer gently, uncovered, about 1 hour or until mixture is translucent and a pale straw colour; stir occasionally during cooking.

4 Stir in rosewater, tint with colouring. Pour and spread mixture into greased deep 19cm square cake pan, stand, uncovered, 3 hours or overnight. Cut jelly into squares using oiled knife.

5 Coat squares in combined sifted icing sugar and extra cornflour.

honey yogurt cake

1 Grease 15cm x 25cm loaf pan, line base with baking paper. Beat butter, yogurt, cinnamon and honey in small bowl with electric mixer until just combined and smooth. Transfer mixture to large bowl.

2 Beat eggs and sugar in small bowl with electric mixer until thick and creamy.

3 Stir egg mixture into yogurt mixture. Fold in sifted flour and baking powder.

4 Spread mixture into prepared pan. Bake in moderate oven about 45 minutes. Stand cake 10 minutes before turning onto wire rack to cool. Serve dusted with combined sifted icing sugar and extra cinnamon.

200g unsalted butter, chopped

¾ cup (180ml) plain yogurt

½ teaspoon ground cinnamon

½ cup (125ml) honey

2 eggs

¼ cup (55g) caster sugar

1¾ cups (260g) self-raising flour

½ teaspoon baking powder

1 tablespoon icing sugar mixture

½ teaspoon ground cinnamon, extra

Beat butter, yogurt, cinnamon and honey until combined and smooth.

Fold flour and baking powder into egg and yogurt mixture.

almond cream with spiced fruit

1 Blend rice flour and sugar with ½ cup (125ml) of the milk in small bowl. Bring remaining milk and rind to boil in medium pan, stir in flour mixture, stir constantly over heat until mixture boils and thickens.

2 Stir in remaining ingredients. Spoon mixture into 6 dishes (¾ cup/180ml capacity); cool. Cover, refrigerate until cold. Serve with spiced fruit.

spiced fruit Place fruit in bowl, cover with water; stand 2 hours. Drain, discard water. Bring measured water, sugar, cinnamon, cloves, liqueur and rosewater to boil in pan, simmer, uncovered, 30 minutes or until syrupy and reduced to about 2½ cups (625ml). Remove from heat, stir in fruit and nuts, cool. Cover; refrigerate 3 hours or overnight.

serves 6

¼ cup (35g) rice flour

¼ cup (55g) caster sugar

3 cups (750ml) milk

½ teaspoon grated lemon rind

¾ cup (90g) ground almonds

¼ cup (35g) slivered almonds

1 tablespoon rosewater

SPICED FRUIT

½ cup (45g) dried apples

¾ cup (110g) dried apricots

½ cup (85g) seedless prunes

1 litre (4 cups) water

¾ cup (165g) caster sugar

2 cinnamon sticks

3 cloves

2 teaspoons Amaretto

1 tablespoon rosewater

¼ cup (30g) chopped walnuts

Bring milk and rind to boil; stir in rice flour mixture until it thickens.

Remove pan of spiced syrup from heat; stir in fruit and nuts.

Cook dates, spices, cream, nuts and rind until dates are soft.

Spread filling on pastry with border on one side; roll from other side.

almond date spirals

5 sheets fillo pastry

40g butter, melted

400g seedless fresh dates, chopped

½ teaspoon ground cinnamon

½ teaspoon ground nutmeg

½ teaspoon ground ginger

½ cup (125ml) cream

½ cup (40g) flaked almonds, toasted

2 teaspoons grated lemon rind

1 Trim a sheet of baking paper to same size as a sheet of pastry, place on bench. Layer sheets of pastry together on paper, brushing each layer of pastry with a little of the butter.
2 Combine dates, spices, cream, nuts and rind in medium pan, cook, stirring, until dates are soft and almost all the cream is absorbed; cool.
3 Spread date mixture over pastry, leaving 4cm border at one long side. Roll pastry from other long side, using paper as a guide. Cover; refrigerate 30 minutes. Cut roll into 1.5cm slices, place cut side up, about 2cm apart on greased oven tray. Bake in moderate oven about 20 minutes or until pastry is crisp.

makes about 25

Crush star anise, cloves, cardamom and coriander in mortar and pestle.

Stir spices, ginger, tea bags, sugar, water and milk until sugar dissolves.

spiced milk tea

1 Using a mortar and pestle, lightly crush star anise, cloves, cardamom and coriander.

2 Combine anise mixture, ginger, cinnamon, tea bags, sugar, water and milk in large pan, stir over heat, without boiling, until sugar dissolves; bring to boil. Strain mixture into jug; serve warm topped with nuts.

makes about 1.75 litres (7 cups)

1 star anise

2 cloves

1 cardamom pod

2 coriander seeds

1 teaspoon ground ginger

1 cinnamon stick, halved

2 jasmine tea bags

½ cup (110g) caster sugar

1 litre (4 cups) water

3 cups (750ml) milk

¼ cup (20g) flaked almonds, toasted, crushed

almond milk

¼ cup (40g) blanched almonds, toasted

¾ cup (180ml) plain yogurt

2 cups (500ml) milk

½ teaspoon ground cinnamon

2 tablespoons caster sugar

6 ice cubes

1 Blend or process nuts until finely chopped.
2 Add remaining ingredients, blend or process until smooth.

makes about 3 cups (750ml)

Blend or process nuts until finely chopped.

Add remaining ingredients, blend or process until smooth.

iced mint tea

1 Combine mint, tea bags, sugar and water in large heatproof bowl, stand 15 minutes.
2 Strain mixture into jug; cool to room temperature. Refrigerate.

makes about 3 cups (750ml)

1½ cups firmly packed fresh mint leaves

3 Chinese green tea bags

2 tablespoons sugar

3 cups (750ml) boiling water

Combine all tea ingredients in heatproof bowl, stand 15 minutes.

Strain mixture into jug; cool to room temperature; refrigerate.

Lightly crush toasted cardamom pods in mortar and pestle.

Stir cardamom, coffee, sugar and water until it reaches boiling point.

cardamom coffee

3 cardamom pods

2 tablespoons coarsely ground dark roasted coffee beans

1 teaspoon sugar

1 cup (250ml) water

1 Place cardamom pods on oven tray. Toast in moderate oven 4 minutes; cool. Using a mortar and pestle, lightly crush pods.
2 Combine cardamom, coffee, sugar and water in small pan, stir over heat until mixture comes up to boiling point; remove from heat.
3 Stand for 1 or 2 minutes to allow coffee grains to settle. Strain into tiny coffee cups to serve.

serves 4

glossary

allspice also known as pimento or Jamaican pepper; so named because it tastes like a combination of nutmeg, cumin, clove and cinnamon – all spices.

ALMONDS

blanched brown skins removed.

flaked paper-thin slices.

ground we used packaged commercially ground nuts.

slivered nuts cut lengthways.

amaretto an almond-flavoured liqueur.

artichoke hearts tender centre of the globe artichoke, itself the large flower-bud pf a member of the thistle family; having tough petals like leaves, edible in part when cooked. Artichoke hearts can be harvested fresh from the plant or purchased canned or in glass jars, in brine.

baking powder a raising agent containing starch, but mostly cream of tartar and bicarbonate of soda in the proportions of 1 teaspoon cream of tartar to ½ teaspoon bicarbonate of soda. This is equal to 2 teaspoons baking powder.

BEEF

chuck steak from neck area.

minced ground.

beetroot also known as red beets; firm, round root vegetable. Can be eaten raw, grated, in salads; boiled and sliced, or roasted then mashed like potatoes.

bicarbonate of soda baking soda.

BREADCRUMBS

packaged fine textured, crunchy, purchased, white breadcrumbs.

stale one- or two-day-old bread made into crumbs by grating, blending orprocessing.

burghul (cracked wheat) wheat that is steamed until partly cooked, cracked then dried. Cracked wheat can be substituted.

butter use salted or unsalted (sweet) butter; 125g equals 1 stick butter.

buttermilk is now made by adding a culture to a low-fat milk to give a slightly acidic flavour; a low-fat milk can be substituted, if preferred.

cajun seasoning a combination of dried ingredients consisting of salt, blended peppers, garlic, onion and spices.

capsicum bell peppers.

celeriac tuberous root with brown skin, white flesh and a celery-like flavour.

CHEESE

cream also known as Philly.

fetta a soft Greek cheese with a sharp, salty taste.

haloumi a firm, cream-coloured sheep's milk cheese. A little like fetta in flavour.

kefalograviera a semi-hard cheese with a smooth texture and a slightly salty aftertaste; made from sheep's milk.

mascarpone a fresh, unripened smooth triple cream cheese with a rich, sweet taste, slightly acidic.

ricotta fresh, unripened light curd cheese.

tasty cheddar matured cheddar; use a hard, good-tasting variety.

chickpeas also known as ceci and garbanzos; ½ cup (100g) dried chickpeas equals a 300g can of chickpeas. Soak dried peas overnight in cold water, drain. Add to pan of water, bring to boil, simmer, covered, 1 hour or until tender.

CHILLIES

Available in many different types and sizes. Use rubber gloves when chopping fresh chillies as they can burn your skin.

bottled hot red whole small red chillies in a vinegar and salt solution.

dried crushed available from supermarkets and Asian food stores.

powder the Asian variety is the hottest, made from ground chillies; can be used instead of fresh chillies in the proportions of ½ teaspoon chilli powder to 1 medium chopped fresh chilli.

coconut use desiccated coconut unless otherwise specified.

colourings we used concentrated liquid vegetable food colourings.

cooking salt a coarse salt (not the same as fine table salt).

corella pear miniature dessert pear up to 10cm long.

cornflour cornstarch.

couscous a fine cereal made from semolina.

CREAM

Fresh pouring cream; has a minimum fat content of 35%.

low fat sour a less dense, commercially cultured soured cream; this cream will not set as firmly as sour cream. It contains 18% milk fat.

thickened (whipping) has a minimum fat content of 35%, plus thickener.

cream of tartar an ingredient in baking powder. It is also sometimes added to confectionery mixtures to help prevent sugar from crystallising.

eggplant aubergine.

fillo pastry also known as phyllo dough; comes in tissue-thin pastry sheets bought chilled or frozen.

FLOUR

rice flour made from ground rice.

white all-purpose flour.

wholemeal plain wholewheat flour without the addition of baking powder.

garam masala a combination of powdered spices, consisting of cardamom, cinnamon, cloves, coriander, cumin and nutmeg in varying proportions. Sometimes pepper is used to make a hot variation.

ghee a pure butter fat available in cans, it can be heated to high temperatures without burning because of the lack of salts and milk solids.

gherkin cucumber a short, slim, rough-skinned cucumber. This variety is mainly used for pickling.

GINGER

fresh, green or root ginger scrape away skin and grate, chop or slice as required.

ground should not be substituted for fresh ginger in any recipe.

green onions also known as scallions, eschalots and green shallots. Do not confuse with the small golden shallots.

green tea bags also known as oolong tea.

herbs we specify when to use fresh or dried herbs. Use dried (not ground) herbs in the proportions of 1:4 for fresh herbs, e.g. 1 teaspoon dried herbs instead of 4 teaspoons chopped fresh herbs.

kataifi packaged, shredded pastry bought chilled; it is available from delicatessens.

LAMB

minced ground lamb.

rack row of cutlets.

shank forequarter leg.

lavash flat, unleavened bread of Mediterranean origin.

lentils dried pulses. There are many different varieties, usually identified and named after their colour.

macadamias Queensland nuts or Hawaiian nuts.

maple-flavoured syrup golden/pancake syrup; honey can be used as a substitute.

mustard seeds can be black or yellow.

OIL

extra virgin and virgin the highest quality olive oils, obtained from the first pressings of olives.

light olive mild-tasting, light in flavour, colour and aroma, but not low in kilojoules.

olive a blend of refined and virgin olive oils, especially good for everyday cooking.

vegetable we used a polyunsaturated vegetable oil.

okra a green, ridged, immature seed pod, also called lady's fingers.

orange flower water concentrated flavouring made from orange blossoms.

paprika ground dried peppers, available sweet or hot.

parsley, flat-leaf also known as continental parsley or Italian parsley.

pine nuts small, cream-coloured soft kernels.

pistachio pale green, delicately flavoured nut inside hard off-white shells. To peel, soak shelled nuts in boiling water for 5 minutes; drain, then pat dry with absorbent paper. Rub skins with cloth to peel.

pomegranate round fruit, the size of a large orange, with thick, leathery red skin. Contains white seeds in pinkish-red, juicy, sweet pulp.

puff pastry sheets frozen sheets of puff pastry made from wheat flour, vegetable margarine, salt, food acid and water.

quince yellow-skinned fruit with hard texture and acid taste.

rocket also known as arugula, rocket is a green salad leaf.

sambal oelek (also ulek or olek) a salty paste made from ground chillies.

sauternes a sweet, golden wine usually served with dessert.

semolina a hard part of the wheat which is sifted out and used mainly for making pasta.

sesame seeds there are two types, black and white. To toast, spread seeds evenly onto oven tray, place in moderate oven for 5 minutes or stir in heavy-based pan over heat until golden brown.

spatchcock small chicken, weighing around 500g.

star anise the dried star-shaped fruit of an evergreen tree, it has an aniseed flavour.

stock 1 cup (250ml) stock is equivalent to 1 cup (250ml) water plus 1 crumbled stock cube (or 1 teaspoon of stock powder). Be aware of the salt and fat content. Stock is also available in cans and tetra packs, but also be aware of their salt content.

SUGAR

We used coarse granulated table sugar, also known as crystal sugar, unless otherwise specified.

brown a soft, fine granulated sugar containing molasses which gives it its characteristic colour.

caster also known as superfine; is fine granulated table sugar.

icing sugar mixture also known as confectioners' sugar or powdered sugar.

pure icing sugar also known as confectioners' sugar or powdered sugar.

sultanas golden raisins.

sweet potato fleshy white root vegetable.

sweetened condensed milk we used canned milk from which 60% of the water had been removed; the remaining milk is then sweetened with sugar.

tagine a round dish with a conical lid; also name of a recipe for meat or vegetable stew with fruit and nuts.

tahini paste made from crushed sesame seeds.

TOMATO

canned whole peeled tomatoes in natural juices.

egg also known as Roma, Italian or plum tomatoes.

paste a concentrated tomato puree used in flavouring soups, stews, sauces and casseroles.

puree canned pureed tomatoes (not tomato paste). Use fresh, peeled, pureed tomatoes as a substitute, if preferred.

vanilla bean dried bean of the vanilla orchid. It can be used repeatedly, simply wash in warm water after use, dry well and store in airtight container.

VINEGAR

balsamic originated in the province of Modena, Italy. Regional wine is specially processed then aged in antique wooden casks to give a pungent flavour.

brown malt made from fermented malt and beech shavings.

white made from spirit of cane sugar.

white wine is based on white wine.

vine leaves we used vine leaves in brine; available in jars and packets.

yeast allow 2 teaspoons (7g) dried yeast to each 15g compressed yeast if substituting.

za'atar seasoning dry blend of roasted sesame seeds, wild marjoram, thyme and sumac; available in Arabic speciality shops.

zucchini courgette.

index

facts & figures

Wherever you live, you'll be able to use our recipes with the help of these easy-to-follow conversions. While these conversions are approximate only, the difference between an exact and the approximate conversion of various liquid and dry measures is minimal and will not affect your cooking results.

METRIC	IMPERIAL
30ml	1 fluid oz
60ml	2 fluid oz
100ml	3 fluid oz
125ml	4 fluid oz
150ml	5 fluid oz (¼ pint/1 gill)
190ml	6 fluid oz
250ml	8 fluid oz
300ml	10 fluid oz (½ pint)
500ml	16 fluid oz
600ml	20 fluid oz (1 pint)
1000ml (1 litre)	1¾ pints

MEASURING EQUIPMENT

The difference between one country's measuring cups and another's is, at most, within a 2 or 3 teaspoon variance. (For the record, one Australian metric measuring cup holds approximately 250ml.) The most accurate way of measuring dry ingredients is to weigh them. When measuring liquids, use a clear glass or plastic jug with the metric markings. (One Australian metric tablespoon holds 20ml; one Australian metric teaspoon holds 5ml.)

DRY MEASURES

METRIC	IMPERIAL
15g	½oz
30g	1oz
60g	2oz
90g	3oz
125g	4oz (¼lb)
155g	5oz
185g	6oz
220g	7oz
250g	8oz (½lb)
280g	9oz
315g	10oz
345g	11oz
375g	12oz (¾lb)
410g	13oz
440g	14oz
470g	15oz
500g	16oz (1lb)
750g	24oz (1½lb)
1kg	32oz (2lb)

HELPFUL MEASURES

METRIC	IMPERIAL
3mm	⅛in
6mm	¼in
1cm	½in
2cm	¾in
2.5cm	1in
5cm	2in
6cm	2½in
8cm	3in
10cm	4in
13cm	5in
15cm	6in
18cm	7in
20cm	8in
23cm	9in
25cm	10in
28cm	11in
30cm	12in (1ft)

HOW TO MEASURE

When using graduated metric measuring cups, shake dry ingredients loosely into the appropriate cup. Do not tap the cup on a bench or tightly pack the ingredients unless directed to do so. Level top of measuring cups and measuring spoons with a knife. When measuring liquids, place a clear glass or plastic jug with metric markings on a flat surface to check accuracy at eye level.

Note: North America, NZ and the UK use 15ml tablespoons. All cup and spoon measurements are level.

We use large eggs having an average weight of 60g.

OVEN TEMPERATURES

These oven temperatures are only a guide. Always check the manufacturer's manual.

	°C (CELSIUS)	°F (FAHRENHEIT)	GAS MARK
Very slow	120	250	½
Slow	140-150	275-300	1-2
Moderately slow	170	325	3
Moderate	180-190	350-375	4-5
Moderately hot	200	400	6
Hot	220-230	425-450	7-8
Very hot	240	475	9

ARE YOU MISSING SOME OF THE WORLD'S FAVOURITE COOKBOOKS?

The Australian Women's Weekly Cookbooks are available from bookshops, cookshops, supermarkets and other stores all over the world. You can also buy direct from the publisher, using the order form below.

TITLE	RRP	QTY	TITLE	RRP	QTY
Almost Vegetarian	£5.99		French Food, New	£5.99	
Asian, Meals in Minutes	£5.99		Get Real, Make a Meal	£5.99	
Babies & Toddlers Good Food	£5.99		Good Food Fast	£5.99	
Barbecue Meals In Minutes	£5.99		Great Beef Cookbook	£5.99	
Basic Cooking Class	£5.99		Great Chicken Cookbook	£5.99	
Beginners Cooking Class	£5.99		Great Lamb Cookbook	£5.99	
Beginners Simple Meals	£5.99		Greek Cooking Class	£5.99	
Beginners Thai	£5.99		Healthy Heart Cookbook	£5.99	
Best Ever Slimmers' Recipes	£5.99		Indian Cooking Class	£5.99	
Best Food	£5.99		Italian Cooking Class	£5.99	
Best Food Desserts	£5.99		Japanese Cooking Class	£5.99	
Best Food Mains	£5.99		Kids' Birthday Cakes	£5.99	
Big Book of Beautiful Biscuits	£5.99		Kids Cooking	£5.99	
Biscuits & Slices	£5.99		Lean Food	£5.99	
Cakes & Slices Cookbook	£5.99		Low-fat Feasts	£5.99	
Cakes Cooking Class	£5.99		Low-fat Food For Life	£5.99	
Caribbean Cooking	£5.99		Low-fat Meals in Minutes	£5.99	
Casseroles	£5.99		Main Course Salads	£5.99	
Celebration Cakes	£5.99		Meals in Minutes	£5.99	
Chicken Meals in Minutes	£5.99		Mediterranean Cookbook	£5.99	
Chinese Cooking Class	£5.99		Middle Eastern Cooking Class	£5.99	
Christmas Book	£5.99		Midweek Meals in Minutes	£5.99	
Christmas Cooking	£5.99		Muffins, Scones & Bread	£5.99	
Cocktails	£5.99		New Finger Food	£5.99	
Cooking for Crowds	£5.99		Pasta Cookbook	£5.99	
Cooking for Friends	£5.99		Pasta Meals in Minutes	£5.99	
Cooking For Two	£5.99		Potatoes	£5.99	
Creative Cooking on a Budget	£5.99		Quick Meals in Minutes	£5.99	
Detox (Sept 05)	£5.99		Quick-mix Biscuits & Slices	£5.99	
Dinner Beef	£5.99		Quick-mix Cakes	£5.99	
Dinner Lamb (Aug 05)	£5.99		Salads: Simple, Fast & Fresh	£5.99	
Dinner Seafood	£5.99		Saucery	£5.99	
Easy Australian Style	£5.99		Sensational Stir-Fries	£5.99	
Easy Curry	£5.99		Short-order Cook	£5.99	
Easy Spanish-Style	£5.99		Sweet Old Fashioned Favourites	£5.99	
Easy Vietnamese-Style	£5.99		Thai Cooking Class	£5.99	
Essential Barbecue	£5.99		Vegetarian Meals in Minutes	£5.99	
Essential Microwave	£5.99		Weekend Cook	£5.99	
Essential Soup	£5.99		Wicked Sweet Indulgences	£5.99	
Freezer, Meals from the	£5.99		Wok, Meals in Minutes	£5.99	
French Cooking Class	£5.99		**TOTAL COST:**	**£**	

NAME

ADDRESS

POSTCODE

DAYTIME PHONE

I ENCLOSE MY CHEQUE/MONEY ORDER FOR £

OR PLEASE CHARGE MY VISA, ACCESS OR MASTERCARD NUMBER

CARD HOLDER'S NAME

EXPIRY DATE

CARDHOLDER'S SIGNATURE

To order: Mail or fax — photocopy or complete the order form above, and send your credit card details or cheque payable to: Australian Consolidated Press (UK), Moulton Park Business Centre, Red House Road, Moulton Park, Northampton NN3 6AQ, phone (+44) (0) 1604 497531, fax (+44) (0) 1604 497533, e-mail books@acpuk.com
Non-UK residents: We accept the credit cards listed on the coupon, or cheques, drafts or International Money Orders payable in sterling and drawn on a UK bank. Credit card charges are at the exchange rate current at the time of payment.
Postage and packing: Within the UK, add £1.50 for one book or £3.00 for two books. There is no postal charge for orders of three or more books for delivery within the UK. For delivery outside the UK, please phone, fax or e-mail for a quote.
Offer ends 30.12.2005

Test Kitchen
Food director *Pamela Clark*
Food editor *Karen Hammial*
Assistant food editors *Kirsty McKenzie, Louise Patniotis*
Test Kitchen manager *Elizabeth Hooper*
Home economists *Emma Braz, Kimberley Coverdale, Kelly Cruikshanks, Nadia French, Sarah Hobbs, Amanda Kelly, Alison Webb*
Editorial coordinator *Rebecca Steyns*

ACP Books
Editorial director *Susan Tomnay*
Creative director *Hieu Chi Nguyen*
Editor *Stephanie Kistner*
Designer *Fiona Thompson*
Design assistant *Karen Lai*
Studio manager *Caryl Wiggins*
Editorial coordinator *Merryn Pearse*
Publishing manager (sales) *Brian Cearnes*
Publishing manager (rights & new projects) *Jane Hazell*
Marketing director *Nicole Pizanis*
Sales and marketing coordinator *Caroline Lowry*
Pre-press *Harry Palmer*
Production manager *Carol Currie*
Business manager *Seymour Cohen*
Business analyst *Martin Howes*
Chief executive officer *John Alexander*
Group publisher *Pat Ingram*
Publisher *Sue Wannan*
Editor-in-chief *Deborah Thomas*
Produced by ACP Books, Sydney.
Printed by Times Printers, Singapore.
Published by ACP Publishing Pty Limited, 54 Park St, Sydney; GPO Box 4088, Sydney, NSW 2001.
Ph: (02) 9282 8618 Fax: (02) 9267 9438.
acpbooks@acp.com.au
www.acpbooks.com.au
To order books, phone 136 116.
Send recipe enquiries to:
recipeenquiries@acp.com.au
AUSTRALIA: Distributed by Network Services, GPO Box 4088, Sydney, NSW 2001.
Ph: (02) 9282 8777 Fax: (02) 9264 3278.
UNITED KINGDOM: Distributed by Australian Consolidated Press (UK), Moulton Park Business Centre, Red House Rd, Moulton Park, Northampton, NN3 6AQ.
Ph: (01604) 497531 Fax: (01604) 497533
acpukltd@aol.com
CANADA: Distributed by Whitecap Books Ltd, 351 Lynn Ave, North Vancouver, BC, V7J 2C4.
Ph: (604) 980 9852 Fax: (604) 980 8197
customerservice@whitecap.ca
www.whitecap.ca
NEW ZEALAND: Distributed by Netlink Distribution Company, ACP Media Centre, Cnr Fanshawe and Beaumont Streets, Westhaven, Auckland.
PO Box 47906, Ponsonby, Auckland, NZ.
Ph: (09) 366 9966 ask@ndcnz.co.nz
SOUTH AFRICA: Distributed by PSD Promotions, 30 Diesel Road Isando, Gauteng Johannesburg.
PO Box 1175, Isando 1600, Gauteng Johannesburg.
Ph: (2711) 392 6065 Fax: (2711) 392 6079
orders@psdprom.co.za

Clark, Pamela.
The Australian Women's Weekly cooking class Middle Eastern

Rev ed.
Includes index.
ISBN 1 86396 460 6

1. Cookery, Middle Eastern.
I. Title: Australian women's weekly.

641.5956

© ACP Publishing Pty Limited 1996
ABN 18 053 273 546

This publication is copyright. No part of it may be reproduced or transmitted in any form without the written permission of the publishers.
First published 1996. Reprinted 2001, 2003.
Revised and updated 2005.